What People Are Saying...

"I love this book because it's true, and its message is inspiring and hopeful. Debbie Gill's life is worth sharing, and I'm glad she did."

— Caroline Myss, author of *Anatomy of the Spirit*

"From the moment I heard Debbie's story, I knew it was worth sharing. Her animated story-telling, coupled with her unique, sometimes outrageous experiences, make this a must-read book."

— Lois Hoffman, author of *Write a Book, Grow Your Business*

"I've known Debbie all her life and have seen the progression of her addiction over the years. I was not only elated but very proud when I saw her work hard to put her disease in remission. She's done an outstanding job taking her recovery to a higher spiritual level, while sharing her experience, strength, and hope with others."

— Father Bill Hultberg, Past Spiritual Advisor at the Caron Foundation

STRUCK
BY
LIGHTNING

My Journey
from the Shadow to the Light

To Jimmy,

May your light always shine !!

Blessings, Debbie Gill

DEBBIE GILL

Copyright © 2018 by Debbie Gill

All rights reserved. This book or any portion thereof may not be reproduced or used in any manner whatsoever without the express written permission of the author except for the use of brief quotations in a book review.

ISBN 13: 978-1-732-6305-0-5

Struck by Lightning is a spiritual autobiography, and the author has recreated events, locales, and conversations recalling them to the best of her ability. She changed some individual names, identifying characteristics, places, and occupations to maintain anonymity for certain people.

Express permission from Caroline Myss has been given to use all the quotes from her work in this book.

Express permission from Father Bill Hultberg has been given to use his poem, Caron Chapel Prayer, in this book.

The Happy Self-Publisher

publish.smile.repeat

happyselfpublisher.com

*I dedicate this book to Don and Pat Gill, my parents, and Father Bill
Hultberg, my uncle; with both love and gratitude
for giving me life and saving it.*

~~~~~~~~

Caron Chapel Prayer

Lord God, I acknowledge you as my
Savior and Redeemer.
I ask you to come into my life.
Send the power of the Holy Spirit upon me,
to enlighten my mind and will
as to what I must do ...
and then move my will to do it!
I ask the Holy Spirit
to heal me of all obsessions
and compulsions
to use alcohol and other drugs
or relationships or behaviors addictively.
Grant that I may never separate
myself from you again,
for you are my Lord and God.
Amen.

Written by Father Bill Hultberg

Table of Contents

Acknowledgments vii

Introduction ix

Little Miss Extrovert 1

The Invisible Child..11

Into the Abyss...19

Sinking Deeper 29

Struck by Lightning 39

Allergic to Alcohol 49

Putting Down the Drink 59

Banging My Head Against a Brick Wall...............................67

Love at First Sight 81

Breakthrough 97

On the Rebound 107

The Honeymoon Phase 121

My Dark Night of the Soul 127

Hitting Rock Bottom...137

I Surrender 149

Spiritual Awakening and Rebirth..159

The 12 Steps and Beyond 173

Leaps of Faith, Manifestations, and Miracles 185

Letting Go of Limiting Beliefs 201

The Healing Path of the Wounded Healer 209

Epilogue 225

Author's Note 227

Bibliography and Recommended Reading 231

Acknowledgments

First, I want to thank God, my Higher Power, who has never abandoned me, even though at times I thought He did. He has always held my soul with tenderness and love, encouraging me to find my truth and purpose in life, while allowing me to make mistakes.

Special gratitude goes to my uncle, Father Bill Hultberg, who saved my life by arranging my admittance to the Caron Foundation, a first-rate drug and alcohol rehabilitation center. Without his love and support, I would not be where I am today. When I was a little girl, he called me Princess; as a young adult, he referred to me as a dry drunk; now, his wisdom and recovery experiences have guided me to a happy, productive life as a sober woman.

Caroline Myss, a huge thank you for providing me the means to develop my inner self-esteem. Your inspiration and wisdom, along with your integrity for truth, have touched my soul and psyche like no other teacher. For my benefit, you took me to task at times, but always with love and compassion. Your kindness and generosity, as well as your encouragement for me to finish this book, will be forever etched on my heart. I will always cherish the moments we've shared.

John Holland, thank you for guiding me to develop my intuition to the level I have. You have been generous and kind with your words. Many of the experiences I describe are a direct result of what you taught me. You have given me a priceless gift, and for that, I am most grateful.

Lois Hoffman, thank you for your support in teaching me how to begin organizing my book. Your six-week course, *Write a Book, Grow Your Business*, gave me the knowledge of how to create an outline, which instilled the motivation for me to move forward. Your reassuring words boosted my confidence to continue.

Thank you, Ray Richardson; your photography is beyond excellent. You have captured my true essence.

Thank you to Julie Willson, from Edits by Julia, for your magnificent work on my book proposal.

Last, but certainly not least, to all my friends and family, who have supported and encouraged me to continue in my efforts: you know who you are, and I love you all very much. Also, thank you to everyone who either came into and then out of my life, threw me a curve ball, or challenged me; without you, I would not have become the person I am today. For where there is darkness, there is also light.

Introduction

Do you ever wonder who you are or what you need to learn about yourself? Do you find yourself doing things, repeating the same pattern, but you don't know the reason why? Do you ever question why you believe the things you do or why your life is the way it is?

The answers to these questions require understanding your archetypal patterns. Once you recognize the behavior pattern, you can understand yourself, and others, better. An archetype is a universal, mythical pattern of power that you, and everyone in the world, are born knowing.

Struck by Lightning: My Journey from the Shadow to the Light is a spiritual autobiography that illustrates my endeavor, from the time of my birth until the present, to uncover the answer to these inspiring questions. My archetypes and their respective patterns of behavior emerge on many occasions and are sprinkled throughout the book, giving rise to opportunities to identify them. Only when you take the steps as I have, are you able to start your journey, learning the specifics of what makes you tick.

It's often at a turning point where you are challenged to make a decision that either helps you grow or prevents you from having authority over your life. At times, one or more of the four Survival archetypes present you with opportunities to develop, or increase, your self-esteem. These archetypes reside in the Survival family: the Child, the Victim, the Prostitute, and the Saboteur; they are universal to every human being and are accompanied by eight additional archetypes that surface at some point. The Addict, the Athlete, the Student, and the Femme Fatale are a few of the eight presented in this book.

All archetypes have aspects of shadow and light. The shadow is not dark or evil but the part of yourself that lies beneath the one you know, your consciousness. These patterns of behavior are often ignored or denied when residing in the shadow and can cause you unnecessary pain and suffering. Remaining in the shadow blocks the path to your empowerment. Once you recognize and face these patterns in the shadow, they become your friends, allowing you to step into the light and integrate them into your spirit or inner self. When you begin to know yourself, you start the journey of moving from the shadow to the light.

Struck by Lightning was written at a time when a cloud of darkness is shrouding the world. This shadow is gripping humanity — from the countless confrontations polarizing social and cultural groups to the addiction to power, money, and sex — and is causing the decline of tolerance, compassion, and most of all, love.

"You must be the change you wish to see in the world" (Mahatma Gandhi).

For the world to shift direction, first there must be a shift in you. I desperately wanted to change but didn't know how. This book is written in chronological order and portrays the trials and tribulations I overcame to be the change. It examines the emotional conflicts and patterns of behavior I experienced throughout life and the consequences that were the result of my choices.

I was born under a veil of darkness that held me in its clutches for years. One by one, the looming shadows of my archetypes surfaced, taking charge of me, leading me down a dark path. At times, they went to war with each other, fighting for control, while on different occasions, the battle waged between the shadow and the light. Unaware of how to escape from these restraints and be the change, I frequently fell into despair, ensuring my worthlessness.

Every single decision made in my history, from the onset of the wounded child, was instrumental and necessary for me on the journey of my life. It was long and arduous, and when I found myself alone, which was more often than not, I questioned God, searching for the way to be the change.

The answer, hidden by my shadows, remained elusive, as I fell into a murky abyss until my final descent into the dark night of the soul. During the dark night, I reached a crisis of faith in myself. When everything I believed in collapsed around me, I stood at a turning point, alone and with nowhere to go. I had to make the most crucial decision in my life: surrender and ask God for help, or die. With this spiritual awakening, the rebirth of my authentic soul, I realized I was walking the healing path of the Wounded Healer.

I was facing the journey of life, which took me from the outside world to the journey behind my eye, not only bringing light to the shadow, but being the change.

My purpose has been revealed: to be the change and be of service to others. In *Struck by Lightning*, I share that no matter where you come from, how severe your circumstances may be, or what you think, it is possible to change. I hope that after reading this book, if there is a familiarity with any thoughts or emotions presented here, a spark is ignited that starts your search to unearth the truth that lies within you. When you do the work, you gain a greater awareness of the person you are today, as well as an appreciation of where you came from. You need this. Your friends and family need this. The world needs this.

What I know for sure is that it's possible for you to become the divine person you were born to be. However, it not only takes strength and courage to delve beneath your surface, unmasking the profound truth that lies within you; it also requires a willingness to heal. You should not take it lightly or casually, and it is best to have someone you trust hold space for you throughout your healing process. We all have wounds, but we don't have to live in them. May the Grace of God be with you and in you.

One final note: To further understand your archetypes and how they affect you, read *Sacred Contracts* by Caroline Myss; the book describes an Archetypal Wheel, where all twelve of your archetypes reside, similar to the twelve houses of the zodiac. In creating your Chart of Origin, each of your archetypes is placed into the house of service it most influences. The Archetypal Wheel is an intuitive tool where you receive symbolic information. To learn more about this medium, there is additional information provided in the Author's Note. Please know it is not necessary to understand this information to follow the story of the book.

CHAPTER 1

Little Miss Extrovert

I am a little extrovert.
~ Kushal Pal Singh ~

I was born a pickle. Yes, you read correctly. Since I was born a pickle, the odds were stacked against me. Other children were born as cucumbers that might or might not ferment into pickles, but I didn't have that choice. I was born an Addict.

It was a pattern of behavior that controlled my life; I was living in the shadow.

In the beginning, our family of four settled into a small brick ranch located in Rolling Hills, a tidy neighborhood comprised of starter homes in Wilmington, Delaware. From early on, the differences between my brother and me were evident; Donnie inherited my mother's intellect and responsibility, while I was more like my father: extroverted and inquisitive.

My father, Don, who at six foot two could be intimidating if not for his dimpled smile, was an industrial engineer for General Motors and spent five years at General Motors Institute to earn his degree. Pat, my mother, was a dainty woman who embodied the characteristics of Betty Crocker: a stay-at-home mom of the 1960s. Donnie, two and a half years my senior, was fair skinned with freckles and very proud to have a little sister. As for me, for the first few years of my life, I resembled the cartoon figure of the roly-poly Michelin Tire man.

During playtime, when I engaged in vigorous play, these traits were easily seen. My energy ran full steam ahead, that is, until there wasn't any left and I just conked out, falling asleep even before the sun went down. My sleeping habits made it difficult for my parents to make regular drop-in visits to relatives. In those days, you didn't telephone ahead; you just stopped by and surprised them.

On the flip side, I always asked to go to bed before my scheduled time. This simplified life for my parents; they never had a bedtime battle with me. Even at such a tender age, just a toddler, if you looked, you could see the beginning of my fermentation. Black-and-white thinking, where there's no gray or in between, may have accelerated my proclivity for addiction.

You could tell I was a rough-and-tumble tomboy by the shoes I wore. Unlike many children my age who outgrew their shoes, mine would be in tatters. My mother found it necessary to buy twice the number of shoes as anyone she knew. More shoes, more play, more sleep, more everything. The "more is better" mentality was already beginning to form, even before I reached the age of consciousness.

~~~~~~~~

When I cast my Chart of Origin from Caroline Myss's Archetypal Wheel (which is divided into twelve houses, similar to the twelve houses of the zodiac, and where you receive symbolic information), the Addict fell in the First House, the one that corresponds to Ego and Personality. Each house in the Archetypal Wheel signifies a different aspect of your life; the archetype that falls in the First House is the most important one; it expresses what you use to build your identity and the persona you show the outside world. In my life, it is the Addict I present, and the one who aids in the discovery of who I am. (See Author's Note.)

~~~~~~~~

Trust is as essential to children in their early years as love, safety, and nurturing are. When broken, even in innocent, naive ways, harmful effects may result. The following scene occurred when I was about two years old and just learning to speak. Although I will never know the full extent this played out in my life, my father felt the need to experiment, and I happened to be the unfortunate target. He wanted to see if I would name two separate foods the reverse of what they were.

In a nutshell, he taught me that a doughnut was a banana and a banana was a doughnut. It wasn't cause for alarm, until one day I was visiting Aunt Gertie. She had a basket of fruit on the kitchen counter, and I asked her if I could have a doughnut. Aunt Gertie told me she didn't have doughnuts. In defiance, I said "Yes, you do," pointing my chubby index finger at the basket. It was only then I learned the truth about bananas and doughnuts.

What was my father thinking?

Just after I turned four, GM transferred my dad to Michigan, and we relocated to Birmingham, a suburb outside of Detroit. We made ourselves comfortable in a cozy, three-bedroom brick ranch nestled in a close-knit community. It was one of the happiest times I can remember.

From an active and fun-loving viewpoint, I was Little Miss Extrovert, enamored with meeting people; everyone was fair game, as I did not discriminate. However, there was one small snag for my bubbly personality: Melrose Avenue was a bustling street, and I was not allowed to cross it. So how was I going to meet my neighbors? After putting on my thinking cap, I came up with a smart idea (at least for a four-year-old).

I decided I would go around the block, knock on everybody's front door, and introduce myself by saying, "Hi, I'm Debbie Gill from Delaware. Who are you?" My parents were blind to my amusing behavior, as they soon discovered one Sunday morning when walking home from Mass at St. Christopher's, located across the street.

Several neighbors were outside gardening or enjoying coffee on their stoops, and when we passed, each stopped to wave, saying, "Hello, Debbie." It wasn't just one or two residents but a handful who greeted me. Since my parents hadn't introduced themselves to anyone yet, this friendliness baffled them.

One of the neighbors noticed the confusion on their faces and explained how we met. My parents chuckled as they relaxed. "Thank goodness," my mother answered back; later, she told me how relieved they both were to know the truth.

During the period we lived in Michigan, not only did the Addict archetype surface, two additional ones did as well: the Student and the Athlete. The Student archetype is interested in learning, loves to learn, and wants to be at the head of the class. This archetype appreciates gaining new knowledge and can't get enough of it. And the Athlete archetype includes the Tomboy, fitting my rough-and-tumble traits perfectly. These are girls who are drawn to the interests and play geared to boys. Athletes are competitors whose passions include winning, fitness, and the sports pages.

The first pattern to emerge and come to life, after I enrolled in full-time kindergarten at age five, was the Student. At the time, the entire school system in the state of Michigan was exceptional, including pre-elementary school. Even in 1963, my teacher, Mrs.

Fischtower, assigned an extensive amount of work to take home and complete. My mother, fortunate not having to work outside the home, spent a considerable amount of time teaching me; I knew the alphabet when I was three and learned to read at age four. Because of my desire to learn and my love for almost any subject, I quickly accomplished the often-challenging material.

Every morning, I woke up excited and eager to go to school and soak up something new. An entirely new world opened up for me, and like a good Addict, I craved more of it, soaking it up like a sponge. One of my homework assignments required me to find, cut, and paste in a notebook five pictures of various objects that began with a particular letter of the alphabet. To complete the task, I had to write (in cursive, not print) a sentence about each item.

In addition to the homework assignments, we had to read a minimum of ten books throughout the year. For the Student, reading more than ten books was a snap. When compared to the homework I was given at St. Mary Magdalen, the school I enrolled in when we moved back to Delaware, first grade was effortless. My parents discussed whether they should advance me to the second grade but didn't because my mother thought I wasn't mature enough emotionally.

The other archetype that surfaced was the Athlete. Although I was too young at the time to participate in athletic sports, I was eager for my dad to take my brother and me to see the Detroit Tigers play in the old Tiger Stadium. He taught us both how to fill out a scorecard with the statistics used for baseball. Here I was, a little five-year-old girl, calculating RBIs and ERAs. I was so addicted to baseball (and later to other sports); impatience mounted as I waited for the next day's paper to arrive, so I could open it to the Sports page and read about the baseball games played the day before, especially those we attended. Furthermore, I compared the statistics in the paper with those I calculated, and they were always identical, compelling me to boast about my mathematical prowess to anyone who would listen. All three archetypes joined forces here: my craving (Addict) for sports (Athlete) and statistics (Student) created an intense passion inside of me.

Let me return to the statement, "I was born a pickle." As I mentioned, it refers to the Addict archetype, an archetype few people are grateful to have. Falling into the minority of these, I appreciate the pattern of power it has, as I have evolved and matured, facing its shadow: powerlessness, a struggle with willpower and the absence of self-control. In *Sacred Contracts*, Myss writes, "People who are extremely intellectual or emotional frequently have a close link to this archetype, because they struggle to balance these powers." After explaining the following archetypal experience that occurs to everyone, you'll understand why it is pivotal to my story.

At the Power of Archetypes workshop in 2013, Myss stated, "An initiation is an archetypal experience that has specific instances or characteristics to it"; she told us we all had it. In many cultures, a turning point usually occurs when a child reaches the age of seven, the ability to tell right from wrong. Myss further says something profound happens at this time; you were given a test when you did something wrong. From ages three to four, you are still unconscious, not knowing right from wrong, and from five to six, you begin to discern whether something is a no-no or is okay. But when you reach age seven, the average age of reason, you become conscious, now knowing the difference between right and wrong.

Several factors occur, starting the moment you did something wrong or told your very first lie. What initially happens is, an adult catches you, who then asks, "Did you do this?" You hear a voice in your head saying, *Tell the truth*. The decision you make at this moment will have an impact on you for life; if you tell the truth, you'll relate it with shame and punishment, making it a painful experience. And if you lie, you'll identify lying with freedom and safety.

When the experience of telling my first lie presented itself, it was premeditated; I was only five years old, an age where conscience is not typically fully formed. But I was not typical. My strategy was well thought out, and I began to execute it. The first step of my plan was to get a paper towel. I politely asked my mother if I could have one, and since it was an unusual request, she asked why I wanted it.

Me at 5 years old

Very innocently, knowing full well I wasn't going to share my intention, I replied, "To wash the car off." I just told my first lie.

Believing what I said was true, my mother handed me a paper towel. There was no forethought in my mind of wiping the car down; however, easing myself to the carport, I gave the car a perfunctory wipe, just in case she was watching.

The next part of my scheme went into action: using it as a gripper to open the can of gasoline. I slowly approached the object of my desire and placed the paper towel over the gas cap. My hand trembled as I deliberately, and with effort, turned it counterclockwise, allowing the sweet scent to escape and permeate my nostrils.

My heart raced, and chills coursed through my body; the battle was on between the Addict's two worthy adversaries: the light (honesty) urged me to stop, telling me what I was doing was dangerous, while the shadow (powerlessness) goaded me to carry on and sniff more gas. The shadow was victorious, and I continued to inhale the noxious fumes, unable to stop.

Finally, after fifteen minutes, lightheaded and dizzy, I managed to screw the lid back on and stand up. Well, sort of. Drunk off the gasoline, I wobbled to the back steps, crawling up the five of them. Pushing open the back door, I teetered throughout the empty house. No one seemed to be home, which left me confused and scared. It wasn't until I neared the front window I saw the reason: everyone was working in the front yard.

Pushing the storm door open, I tripped over my feet and rolled off the porch into the thorny rose bushes. My parents, rushing over to help me, smelled the gasoline as they approached. The last thing I remember is hearing them cry out, "What did you do?" before waking up in the hospital, where they took me for observation.

When we returned home, I knew I was in trouble. But because my parents were more concerned about any harmful side effects from absorbing the gas than in the lie I told, they never punished me. They sat me down and explained to me just how dangerous it was.

The effects of gasoline intoxication listed on the website alcoholrehab.com stated, "The hydrocarbons in gasoline, when inhaled, depress the central nervous system creating a state equivalent to alcohol intoxication. The fumes enter the lungs, and from there, into the bloodstream and on up to the brain. Users of this inhalant can typically experience euphoria, dizziness, lack of coordination, disorientation, slowed down reflexes, and more."

The gravity of the situation I put myself into registered, putting the fear of God in me. I knew I did something wrong and promised never to do it again. Even though I never inhaled gasoline again, the Addict would surface, after lying dormant for seven years, and become more destructive than ever.

CHAPTER 2

The Invisible Child

She's an invisible girl who doesn't want to stand out.
She just wants to be heard without having to shout.
~ Breanna Stockham ~

In 1964, the summer after I turned six, my family returned to Delaware. It seems my mother put her foot down; she was expecting her third child in late December and was not moving to San Diego, where GM wanted to transfer my father. She wanted to be with family when this baby was born. Therefore, Daddy resigned from a distinguished career and was pressured to search for a new job opportunity. We began packing for the relocation, and all I can remember is that I did not want to go.

I loved it in Michigan; these were my most exciting years. They were the only years I knew at the time, but heck, I still enjoyed them. Leaving my friends was a painful experience; my eyes welled, overflowing as I waved goodbye from the car until I couldn't see them anymore. Like many children in my circumstance, it felt as if my life was over.

My parents had flown to Delaware some months before to explore various neighborhoods and places of residence. They settled on a small development under construction, Chapelcroft, blueprinted for fifty-six homes. They determined it to be perfect for their growing family.

We arrived in early August to an unfinished house, leading us to temporarily stay at a local hotel, the El Capitan, until settling in October. My father, still with GM until his notice went into effect, traveled extensively, with an occasional weekend return. Because the hotel was close to St. Mary Magdalen, our new school, it was convenient for my mother, who was seven months pregnant, to drive us back and forth.

Living in such a confined space spawned flaring tempers. Whether I inherited my father's appetite for teasing or learned it, I frequently provoked my older brother. Pick, pick, pick. With his boiling point reached, and his calm demeanor snapped, he began to punch me with his fists.

Crying hysterically, I shouted to my very pregnant and visibly shaken mother to stop him from hitting me. As she pried us apart, guilt set in; I knew this was the last situation she needed, and she told us so. Because we both were at fault, the usual punishment was doled out: standing with our noses against the wall for fifteen minutes. I thought a spanking would be better; it didn't last as long.

My teacher was Sister Trinitas, and eager to please her, I offered to stay and help clean the chalkboard and erasers. The work was straightforward and easily understood, making it simple for the Student archetype. Unaware at the time that I suffered from ADHD with impulsivity, I quickly grew bored and became impetuous, talking in class at inappropriate times, which landed me in the corner more than once.

Finally, October 30 was closing day; we were now able to move into our new home. It was a two-story colonial on half an acre, plenty of room for outside activity, and much larger than our previous residences. Even though I should have been excited about our new house, along with Halloween the next day, happiness escaped me; my dad was away on one of his continental commutes for GM, and I missed him dearly.

For a first-night feast, my mother planned to serve filet mignon for dinner. However, she almost burned the house down when she didn't notice fat dripping onto the flames, igniting them. Black smoke and soot filtered through the air. Mommy quickly scooted my brother and I outside; however, I could still catch a glimpse of dark greasy ashes landing on the counter, curtains, tables, and anything else impeding its progress. Mommy extinguished the fire by tossing handfuls of baking soda on the tenderloins. We were safe, but there was a messy cleanup and a ruined dinner.

The weekends over the next two months were utilized to prepare the nursery for the arrival of the new baby. The idea of being a big sister sent joy through me; I couldn't wait to hold, feed, and play with my little brother or sister. At the end of December, just before Christmas, Mommy's contractions started, so Daddy dropped Donnie and me off at Aunt Dot and Uncle Pinky's on the way to the hospital.

Early the following morning, before school, the phone rang, and Aunt Dot answered. She gave the phone to Donnie and then to me. My entire world collapsed, as I heard my father say, "Debbie, Michael died. Baby Michael died."

"No, no, no," I cried. "It can't be true. There must be a mistake."

It was my first experience with death. Later, I discovered he was born healthy but developed respiratory distress and died the day after his birth, just like JFK's son, Patrick, did.

He told me it was true and said I needed to be a good little girl for Mommy because it was going to be hard for her when she came home. His death crushed me unbelievably. My heart was breaking in two—tears rolled down my cheeks, staining them. As the anger welled up inside of me, I wanted to crawl into a hole and hide. I had no idea what to do with this emotion, and since no one sat me down to guide me through the grieving process, I held it in and became a stuffer, a pattern that lasted decades.

We did not go to school that day. Sister Trinitas was notified and had the entire class pray for my family and me. In the coming days, weeks, and years, I would need a lot more than prayers to help me survive and become the person I was born to be. The hospital released Mommy two days before Christmas, and the death of baby Michael nullified the joy brought from the birth of Jesus.

Christmas wasn't merry that year or for the next several. All my mother did was lay on the sofa and cry. The nursery, beautifully decorated and ready for new life, sat empty and cold, with the door closed, leaving everything as it was. Since my parents didn't speak about Michael's death, I didn't talk about him, either. Although there wasn't a funeral, Mommy and Daddy thought I was too young to cope with the service at All Saints Cemetery, which caused my anger to flare. Not knowing how to release it in a healthy manner, I held that in, as well.

The combination of anger and sorrow began to intensify within me, yet as a six-year-old child with no grief counseling, I was confused and felt isolated, if not invisible, much of the time. Michael's passing was the elephant in the room; no one ever vocalized the pain they suffered because of his death.

It wasn't until the following Christmas that the topic was even brought up, and that happened when my mother opened her gift: a sterling silver charm bracelet with a boy, a girl, and an angel attached. She couldn't contain her tears and softly wept most of the evening.

I wanted to shout, "But I'm here, Mommy! Can't you see me?"

What are children to do when they have no means to express their fears, grief, and other feelings? I had no idea but knew I pushed them away, so I didn't feel anything at all. According to the psychologytoday.com/blog, "The Invisible Power of Childhood Emotional Neglect," "A child who receives any type of message, such as, 'Your feelings don't matter'; or when a child feels sad, and her parents don't ask her, 'What's wrong?', will naturally adapt by pushing her feelings down and away, so they are not visible to others. She may push them so far away they are not visible even to herself."

I learned to wear masks to hide my feelings, and the first one I donned, since Mommy was unable to ease her sorrow, was the Strong Mask. This mask equipped me with the strength to carry on as if nothing happened. It complemented the Look Good Mask that I inherited; everything looked good on the outside but was dying inside. Wearing masks began the ripple effect of unraveling my authentic self, as I put on the People Pleaser, doing whatever it took so others, especially my parents, would accept and be happy with me. When they needed me to be the good little girl, I wore the Look Good Mask.

Another way I dealt with the pain of being the Wounded/Invisible Child, one of the Four Survival archetypes Caroline Myss writes about in *Sacred Contracts*, was to pour myself into school work. The Student archetype helped me navigate through the troubled waters of my home life. Since I loved to learn, the first thing I did when I got home from school was my homework. Even when the days were short and my mother encouraged me to play outside for the small window of daylight left, I wanted to complete my assignments first.

The wounds of the Invisible Child were always present, but several significant moments in my life stand out. There were the occasional happy incidents, such as when I was six years old and won a hundred dollars in the church raffle (this was 1964), or when Happy the Clown drew my name on television, stating I won two tickets to the Ringling Brothers Circus. These were random moments of delight, yet I yearned for something deeper: I wanted my humor, intelligence, or athletic ability to be recognized.

In short, I struggled with the need to be seen. I had to be the best, the fastest, the smartest; if I weren't, I would pout, become depressed, and withdraw. The push/pull and up/down of my life created an inner turmoil I wasn't equipped to handle. Two activities my parents suggested for me included ballet (which I hated, only lasting only a year) and clarinet (which I hated even more, not to mention I had a three-year commitment to it). I hated them because I struggled with them.

In the sixth grade, my competitive streak overshadowed my sensibility when we had a competition in gym class for chin-ups and sit-ups. Beating all the girls wasn't an issue for me; I knew I could do that. My goal was to do more than all the boys in my class, and after doing sixty sit-ups and fifty-five chin-ups, I did. The next day, however, found me doubled over in abdominal pain so bad I could hardly walk.

That competitive streak continued to grow in the eighth grade, as the Athlete physically came forth, and by developing my endurance and willpower, I pushed myself to be the fastest runner in the entire school. I had a year of track and field under my belt, and now it was my time to be the captain. After competing in the trials, I was not only the fastest but also leapt the farthest distance in the long jump. It marked a high point in my young athletic career.

St. Mary Magdalen competed in track and field in the Catholic Youth Organization (CYO) with other parochial schools in the district. My dad, more so than my mother, would come to most of my track meets to cheer me on. I was my father's daughter, and I wanted to make him proud and did so because we usually won.

Two of the most humiliating experiences that chiseled at my self-esteem, lasting for many years, are etched in my memory. The first ordeal occurred during the last event in the semifinals: the 4 × 100 relay. Because I was the Usain Bolt on the team, I held the anchor position. The stress level was high; we needed to win to make it to the finals. Susan, the third runner, handed the baton to me, and I dropped it. Panic set in; I knew it was over, but I immediately picked it up and began to run. Unfortunately, I wasn't fast enough to close the gap, and we lost.

I not only let myself down, I also ruined the future for all my teammates. It wasn't their fault; the first three runners outpaced all the other team's sprinters. Everyone told me how proud they were when I continued to finish the race, but their uplifting words meant little to my deflated self.

Following that debacle, the Artist made an appearance just in time for the class play. Coveting the lead role, I did everything I could to be victorious over the other girl auditioning for the part. The need to be the center of attention led me to become Venus, the Greek goddess in *The Last Mrs. Paris*, an appropriate role for the Femme Fatale, an archetype Caroline Myss told me years later that I had. I landed the part.

We presented the play for the entire school, as well as for the A. I. DuPont Children's Hospital, perfectly and without a hitch. The third time, however, was not always a charm. As part of the CYO Competition, once again, I failed to perform at the expected level.

The scene where I flubbed my lines began when I was to engage in a flirtatious rapport with Mr. Paris. Just as I began to cozy up to him, I looked out to the audience. All of a sudden I saw a burst of light; my father had taken a Polaroid flash photo of me. I was blinded, like a deer in headlights, and unable to remember my lines, but ad-libbed to the best of my ability.

Me, as Venus, in the flirtatious scene with Mr. Paris

To add insult to injury, the prompter, whose job was to provide cues to an actor in a play, had gone AWOL; she had been flirting with the best-looking boy in class. But she wasn't the one in the spotlight, nor was she aware of the emotional upheaval I felt, as once again, it was my fault we lost the competition. The judges made note that my improvisation, while apparent, was as best as possible. Again, the words meant little to me; I felt my confidence shatter into tiny pieces, like shards of glass.

These chinks in my armor, the eating away of my self-esteem, along with my compelling need to be seen, became the threshold of my use of alcohol and drugs. Not even when my father said with conviction, "You have everything in the world going for you," did it prevent me from sliding down into the darkness. How could it, when I thought at the time it wasn't true?

Little did I know just how dark it would get.

CHAPTER 3

Into the Abyss

It is by going down into the abyss that we recover the treasures of life. Where you stumble, there lies your treasure.
~ Joseph Campbell ~

My first experience smoking marijuana took place over the summer of 1970, when I was twelve and just finishing the seventh grade. Jeff, an older friend of my brother's, introduced me to the drug. A few of his friends thought I was cool and were okay with me hanging out with them, although Donnie thought otherwise. I was his kid sister, too immature for his circle of friends.

On this standout day, however, Jeff's intention took precedence. He led me to an open field with tall grasses, where we sat down, making ourselves comfortable. We didn't speak as he carefully pulled out a baggie full of pot and began to roll a joint. His rolling experience was impressive, and he finished in seconds, handing me the cigarette to light before I could say a word.

I inhaled deeply, struggling to hold in the choking smoke. It was too much for me, however, and I began to cough. Jeff smiled and offered me the joint once more, suggesting that I inhale slower. Following his direction, the smoke floated down my lungs, and I quickly felt my emotions deepen, creating a false sense of reality. After we finished the joint, my legs trembled as I stood up. The Addict was awakening after a seven-year hibernation, eager and ready to start a decade of total control and bondage.

It was the era of sex, drugs, and rock and roll. My role models included Janis Joplin, Jimi Hendrix, and Jim Morrison from the Doors. These musicians were incredibly talented. However, their demons had gotten the best of them, and they succumbed to early deaths by overdosing on drugs and alcohol.

Many of my peers deemed themselves invincible. Although I included myself in this group, I set my standards high, choosing not to drink or engage in sexual behavior at such an early age, but smoking a joint now and then seemed harmless. If I could have only seen the error of my ways, I would have made different decisions.

My first experience with alcohol, other than the occasional sip of beer or crème de menthe from my father, came two years after my introduction to marijuana. One summer night, my brother was sneaking out of the house and asked whether I wanted to join him. He was meeting others at a friend's house, who had an in-ground pool, a tree house, and a finished basement with a built-in Bose stereo system and pool table.

Eager to hang out with the cutest boy in the neighborhood, I climbed out my bedroom window to the porch overhang, slid down the column, and met up with Donnie by the pool. Someone offered me a can of beer, which I readily accepted, promptly cracking the tab. The first swallow was palatable, so I quickly gulped down the remaining suds.

The effects of the alcohol started within twenty minutes — I was off to the races. The pickle I was born began to ferment further, and I became drunk as all get-out. I had the urge to kiss everything — the potted red geraniums, the water in the pool, even my brother's cheek.

A bottle of Spanada, an inexpensive Spanish wine, sat on the coffee table, and one of the boys poured me a glass. After several extremely unpleasant sips, I set the glass down. Within ten minutes, I found myself on the verge of vomiting and managed to reach the toilet just in time. This adverse reaction was a huge red flag, warning me to stop this behavior. Unfortunately, its appeal was as addictive as a slot machine, and now I was playing a game of chance with my life.

My brother taught me the art of sneaking out, and I frequently acted on my own, letting myself in after my mother left for work. On one occasion, however, my foolish behavior had shattering consequences that would haunt me for the next twenty years and was the doorway of my descent into the abyss.

That fateful night, I climbed out the window as I had many times before, sliding down the post until my feet touched the ground. A huge party was raging in Devon, a development just a five-minute walk across Shipley Road. By the time I arrived, everything was in full swing—the beer and liquor flowed freely, the music was blaring, and the aroma of marijuana wafted through the air.

The rock and roll seemed to get louder as I tapped the top of my beer can and cracked the tab. "Down the hatch," I announced to no one in particular before guzzling that first beer, eager to secure the buzz that helped make it easier for me to fit in. Within half an hour, I was tuned up.

A short time later, Pitbull, a teen who wasn't enrolled in my high school but hung out there, approached me. He mentioned that there was another party upstairs and led me up to one of the bedrooms. What I found instead was an empty room.

I was angry at being misled, but when I turned to leave, I felt myself being pulled back with a force so powerful it frightened me. My heart began pounding, activating the fight-or-flight response, and panic set in as he flung me roughly onto the bed.

The more I struggled to free myself, the more violent Pitbull became. His intention was crystal clear, and my panic turned to terror in an instant. *This can't be happening*, I thought as I felt his hand fumbling with my belt buckle. Every effort I made to push his body off mine was futile; he was much too powerful. Tears welled up and spilled down my cheeks when I realized my fate: I was about to lose my virginity through a violent and forceful rape.

After he finished, there was a heavy silence, and then he cast me to one side like a discarded piece of trash. Pitbull quickly dressed, strolled out of the room, and left me lifeless on the bed. The devastation of this vile act spread throughout every cell in my body, growing in intensity as the truth of what had just occurred emerged.

In a daze, I told myself the assault had ruined me — *ruined me*. This thought weighed heavily as I quickly pulled my pants on and left the party, too ashamed to look anyone in the eyes. They all knew. Everyone knew what had just taken place, and not one person did anything to help me.

During the walk home, I broke down from both the physical and emotional pain. *It was all my fault*, I thought. *It was wrong to sneak out of the house, to drink and smoke pot. I put myself in this situation; I'm to blame for what happened. I made my bed — now I must lie in it.*

Of course, it wasn't my fault. But since my family never spoke about such topics, I was ignorant of that fact. All I knew was the cross felt overwhelming to bear, and I wanted to crawl into a hole and die. I didn't want to feel this torment. I didn't want to feel this guilt, this shame. In fact, I didn't want to feel *anything*. The desire to feel no emotion, bad or good, was the impetus for the path I chose to walk—a life that was hell on earth, a deep, dark, and empty abyss where I didn't live, I merely existed.

This despicable, life-changing moment created an empty shell of a teenager who already was dealing with wounds from childhood. The effect was paralyzing, and many signs of sexual abuse became evident: PTSD, depression, anger, alcohol and drug abuse, and promiscuous behavior. It led me to search for ways to lessen the pain, if not entirely wipe the event from my memory.

The Addict began to exert greater influence on me as I began to withdrawal from schoolmates, yet desperately wanting to spend time with bad boys that showed me attention. Alcohol, my drug of choice, enabled me to disconnect from my emotions. However, I soon discovered a vast array of barbiturates (or downers), which I swallowed simultaneously, resulting in a synergistic effect.

Quaalude 714s created the greatest euphoria, while Tuinal (tooies), Nembutal (yellow jackets), and Seconal (reds) weren't far behind. They made me feel void of emotion, numb, and withdrawn—my new mission. Every day, I would follow the same pattern: wake up and get ready for school, pop a 'lude or a tooie, and go to class.

Once when I was in typing class and under the influence of a Quaalude, I typed myself right off the chair and onto the floor. Teachers were either clueless or tolerant of such behavior, because it was never acknowledged but was oh, so obvious.

After school, I continued the downhill spiral by stealing my father's whiskey and locking myself in my bedroom, where I would mix it with Tab. The taste was terrible, but the effect was heaven. Feeling the alcohol shield my open wound, I would open my journal and write poems, as the Artist archetype surfaced. I wrote about love—the one emotion I longed for but which eluded me.

Why didn't my mother love me? What had I done wrong? I was unaware at the time that her parents abandoned her at the age of four, which resulted in her inability to give me something she'd never had: a mother's love and nurturing.

Writing about the profound loss I sustained, I felt hollow, almost barren. It was true: I hated myself. Every drink I poured down, every pill I swallowed, pulled me further down into the dark, unable to honor my soul. Did I even have a soul?

Surely God was not pleased with me and might even have despised me, for He had abandoned me. Where was love when I craved it the most? Feeling deprived of this emotion so essential to the human psyche, I desperately clung to any form of love I could find, and sex was the most accessible and obvious choice. Consequently, I engaged in a great deal of promiscuous behavior, which increased in direct proportion to my consumption of alcohol and drugs.

During this disconnected and dismal phase of my life, I lived for one thing and one thing only—school. The Student archetype was an energetic force that came to my rescue more than once. Learning was like a drug to me; I couldn't get enough. Everything I studied I attacked with resolve, be it science, mathematics, or English literature.

It was this year, the year I slid into the abyss, when a sculptor named Rodin touched my soul, striking a chord, if only for a brief moment. One of the assignments in ninth grade history class was to write a report on our favorite artist from the realism era. My project covered Rodin's *The Thinker*, and I composed the essay entirely in poem format, momentarily allowing me to get outside myself. History captivated me, especially when it related to the arts. Not only was the Student archetype prevalent, but the Artist was maturing as well.

Another creative vision came to light in English class. The task involved choosing a partner, and together we were to produce a mini-scene from a favorite English literature book and perform it in full costume. After a friend had agreed to work with me, we selected Lewis Carroll's *Alice's Adventures in Wonderland*. My friend played the role of Alice, while I took on the blue caterpillar character, sitting on a mushroom, smoking a hookah. We asked permission to take the drama outside and converted a student desk into a mushroom. I sat upon the mushroom with my hair rolled into a turban and using my blue bong as the hookah. With slow, deliberate breath, I asked, "Who … are … you?" And for just a brief moment, the extinguished light within me flickered ever so faintly.

As the year unfolded, events occurred that only deepened my pain, both physically and emotionally. Before the life-changing trauma that had taken place, the Athlete archetype had played a dynamic role in my early development, hinting at potential success as a sprinter. The path I went down was far different than the possible one to the Olympics. I was, however, still a rough-and-tumble tomboy wanting to show off my prowess.

Grandiosity often leads to misfortune, as I discovered firsthand after attempting a backflip on the school trampoline, only to land headfirst on the gym floor. The aftermath of this foolish antic was a concussion. Not long after this incident, I suffered another preventable injury while experimenting on the uneven parallel bars, after losing my hold on a reverse grip to the upper bar. Bam! I fell on my heels with such force that both my ankles dislocated. Fortunately, as I sat there writhing in extreme pain, someone rushed over and pushed one of my ankles back into place. The school nurse, who happened to be working late, came to the gymnasium and attended to my needs, providing me with crutches and orders to follow up with my health care provider.

When I arrived home, I was annoyed that my mother wasn't there to help me as I hobbled to the sofa. Just as I settled myself, Paul, a senior at Concord High School I often hung around with, came to visit. You could say I dated him, although I was too young to date: I was only fourteen, although I appeared much older. After several minutes, he noticed my mother wasn't home and began to touch me inappropriately. Just as quickly as I said no, and despite my pain, his hands were around my neck, squeezing with such force that it was hard to breathe. I felt the life begin to drain out of me as I fought to loosen his grip. Even as fear and panic shifted into overdrive from lack of oxygen, I was determined to live. Just as the fight-or-flight response kicked in, releasing a large dose of adrenaline throughout my body, he released his chokehold. I gasped, precious air filling my empty, burning lungs.

Despite my shock and the throbbing pain in my ankle, I managed to sit up. Still dazed and confused, I was grateful that Paul was out the door before I had to say a word. During the brief period between the assault and his departure, I felt my heart begin to tear apart slowly into shreds and gradually sink, like the *Titanic*. My emotional trauma was as sharp as the iceberg piercing the steel hull of the ship. Confused about what had just happened, I began to feel as if somehow I were to blame, questioning what actions of mine had caused this unexpected, unwarranted assault.

I was in a permanent state of melancholy and isolation. Writing about love — the scarcity of it, as well as my yearning for it — temporarily eased my suffering. The Addict was evolving into a beast that controlled not only my physical being but my emotional and spiritual essence, as well. The greater my heartache, the more I reached for anything that would alleviate that hollow feeling in the pit of my stomach. Blinded to the potential perils that lay before me, I was well on my way to a long, dangerous downward spiral. I just didn't realize how deeply I would sink.

CHAPTER 4

Sinking Deeper

When the darkness gets easier, you know you're sinking deeper,
becoming dead yourself.
~ Lucy Christopher ~

The few happy times in my life were interwoven among the many darker ones. One of those bright spots occurred on a three-generation family trip to Curacao, a Caribbean island that is part of the Netherland Antilles, which happened to fall on my fifteenth birthday. For me, the excitement magnified when I discovered my birthday was the same as Queen Julianna of the Netherlands. It was a national holiday, and the entire island, decorated lavishly with colorful lights and showy flowers, celebrated. It felt like the country was throwing me the biggest birthday bash of my life.

To commemorate the occasion, we dined at an upscale restaurant, where I donned a long dress bearing a white bodice with a pleated, red-checked skirt. Beaming, as if I were the source for all the pomp and circumstance, I reveled in the attention, satisfying my need to be seen. Another light would shine on me, however, that left me with an unhinged feeling.

The ogling of thirty-three-year-old Sonny Green, owner of the hotel-casino, made me feel like a woman rather than a young teenager. I had just spent a couple of hours sunbathing when I decided to cool off and jumped into the pool. Lost in my thoughts underwater, I was taken by surprise when Sonny dove in, swam up to me, and firmly embraced me. His actions rattled me, and my response was to slither away, which was effortless because of the baby oil I applied a few minutes earlier.

Sonny's demeanor shifted when he became aware I was underage; he became not only apologetic but respectful; he looked past my parents and requested permission from my grandparents to take my brother and me to the circus. Charmed by his gallantry, they freely gave it.

If they only knew what lurked in the wake of that dignified behavior, I doubt they would have consented. It was true; we did go to the circus, but it was one that was a bit risqué, with scantily clad women. Afterward, we returned to the room Donnie and I shared and sat out on the balcony. As we enjoyed the view, Sonny pulled out a joint he described as highly potent Panama Red; the Addict was overjoyed and needed only two hits to get stoned.

As he was leaving, he handed us a baggie full of the cannabis as a gift. We knew it was too much for us to smoke and way too dangerous to smuggle through customs, so we ditched what remained. The decision was a prudent one; Donnie, with his long hair and hippie attire, attracted lots of attention and had his suitcase searched.

Summer came, and along with it, more egregious behavior on my part, as I fell into a comfortable routine of climbing out my window in the middle of the night. One night remains memorable: the only time I consumed LSD. The same group of ne'er-do-wells from high school, including myself, gathered in a field early one morning to party. Someone handed me half of an orange tablet and told me to swallow it, and without question, I did.

Within a short time, I was dazzled by the fluorescent strings that appeared in front of me. I began to pull them off my arms like a conductor orchestrating a symphony. Gradually drawing the mesh into a peak, much like a crescendo in a musical passage, I gracefully dropped it to the ground. Entirely in a world of my own, it didn't dawn on me that I was hallucinating and that no one else could see it.

When the sun rose, we meandered down Shipley Road heading to my house, pausing to rest on white fence posts bordering the road. Whoa. They appeared to tip over as we leaned against them, but in reality, they were quite sturdy on the ground.

We waited until my mother left for work and all was clear before making our way into the house. As we settled in the living room, I put Uriah Heep's *Demons and Wizards* on the stereo. It was apparent I was still hallucinating because one of the lampshades suddenly shot up and crashed into the ceiling, while our two blue Queen Anne's chairs were dancing.

Exhausted and confused, I had enough and promptly ushered my guests out the door, went upstairs, and collapsed onto the bed. Immediately falling into unconsciousness, I was awakened later in the evening by my concerned mother. After letting her know I wasn't feeling well, which was the absolute truth, I fell back to sleep. In toto, I slept a solid seventeen hours. It wasn't until a few weeks later that I discovered I had ingested half of a four-way Orange Sunshine tab, twice what one person would consume.

In high school, I began to smoke marijuana on a regular basis, up to seven times a day, as it was easier to obtain than alcohol. On a typical day, I would smoke a bowl on the way to school, once or twice during school hours, and then a few more times after school. Although I didn't experience blackouts, the

Addict's pull to escape reality was just as substantial, with the benefit of recalling my actions.

During my sophomore year, I had an extreme case of the "fuck-its." One regret, which anchored me with psychic weight for years and was a direct result of the unhealthy choices I made to smoke cigarettes and pot, was not being able to participate in track and field because I lacked the endurance.

At the time, the Athlete archetype was knocked unconscious by the Addict, squandering all my talents, pushing them to the bottom of life's barrel. And I had talent. I was the youngest girl to win a gold medal in the Junior Olympics, and my father recognized my potential to earn a place on the US Olympic Team as a sprinter.

His intuition was accurate; in eighth grade, I was faster than a girl in the class below who eventually competed in three Olympic trials, placing fourth in one of them. The Athlete, however, was not dead. It would evolve and resurface later in my life.

Just making it through the day required enormous effort. Wearing a mask to hide behind controlled every aspect of my life, and it was exhausting, as I found it necessary to adjust them according to the situation I faced. I hated myself, I hated my actions, and I hated my reputation. Because of this self-hatred, I pretended to be someone other than myself for the approval of others.

Alcohol and drugs intensified my ability to conceal the wounds of the Invisible Child and the sexual trauma that led to my being stuck, emotionally, at fourteen. Unable to process the torment of the assault, the pain grew into a toxic energy that eroded my inner being.

My self-confidence, my essence, my nature, and even my soul were all being devoured by an evil, constant force. The only coping mechanism I knew to handle these demons was to repress my feelings through substance abuse. This bottling up of my emotions was my saving grace, in that I was protected from a complete breakdown or, worse, suicide, but also my worst nightmare, adding to the buildup of internal emotional turbulence.

When I was a senior, purchasing alcohol at the tavern behind Concord High was a regular activity. Everyone relied on me to buy their beer or liquor. One event, the annual ski trip to Stowe, Vermont, called for me to take orders for Molson Golden Ale, where I found it necessary to make two separate purchases. Demand far exceeded the four cases from the first run, so I returned for an additional six cases.

In all, we loaded ten cases of beer onto the bus, rewarding the popular students, who earned the privilege to board. Since I was the go-to girl, it was an automatic pass for me. Also wanting to make every effort to impress, I brought along my bong with some hash to share.

We had the audacity to sit directly behind the bus driver and took turns inhaling the potent resin. Rock and roll music blared on the bus, increasing everyone's desire to partake in serious partying. We drank enough beer to fill the lavatory, and the bus driver found it necessary to stop and empty it twice.

Such raucous behavior, not tolerated in today's world, continued to play out the entire weekend, both on and off the ski slopes. Groups would form together, smoking pot before skiing, and then imbibe in après-ski libations; everyone enjoyed the revelry of a great party.

As a teenager, I never considered the danger of skiing under the influence until I crashed at the top of Mt. Mansfield, a three-and-one-half-mile-long ski run. There were three sharp turns at the peak, followed by a lengthy, unbroken trail, sprinkled with moderate moguls. These bumps allowed me to hone my balance and edging skills necessary for parallel skiing.

Pins and needles morphed into a pure adrenaline rush, as the shadow aspect of my Athlete archetype, with its false sense of invulnerability, hopped off the ski lift and braced for the challenge that lay ahead.

Adjusting my goggles, I slipped my hands through the straps, gripped the poles, and pressed on. Gliding my right ski first, followed by my left, my speed increased. Within seconds, the first curve appeared, and although I cut the edges with ease, I lacked the necessary expertise to reign in my acceleration.

Alarm bells sounded as I lost control at the second 180-degree turn and fell forward, striking my head against the top of the ski pole. The motion forced me to tumble forward, somersaulting several times, unable to catch sight of anything other than white powder. My lungs began to burn from a lack of oxygen; a mouthful of snow prevented me from breathing. *Please, help me, God*, I thought.

I came to an abrupt stop. The duration of my wipeout felt much longer than the few seconds it was. Shaking cobwebs from my head, I assessed the damage: a protruding knot on my forehead, later diagnosed as a concussion, and one ski pole bent in half. Passing skiers stopped to offer aid, but I was determined to ski down the mountain, bent ski pole and all. Still woozy from the fall, it was a daunting task, but I persevered, skiing the final three miles without further incident.

Trouble followed me into the spring on one April afternoon, when a liquor control officer arrested me as I carried out a six-pack of Michelob from the tavern behind my high school. Ironically, the beer wasn't even for me; it was a favor for two friends of mine. After placing me in a pair of matching silver bracelets, one of the officers from the Delaware Alcoholic

Beverage Control (ABC) informed me they were monitoring the establishment for underage patrons.

The other officer asked me if I used a fake ID to make my purchase, and I told him the truth, answering no, I didn't. However, I did have my friend's ID from the University of Delaware, which I turned over with a trembling hand. After examining the ID, he handed it to his partner to check out, telling me I was good enough to pass for it and they would have let me go had I shown it. *Are you kidding?* Irritated by my honesty, I found myself at the age of seventeen, arrested for underage purchase of alcohol. Not only did I have to answer to my parents but also to the court system, for the first of my three arrests, all alcohol-related.

Knowing my parents were very lenient did little to temper my anxiety. Feeling like an actual criminal, I reluctantly called them to bail me out. Since I was still a juvenile, under the age of eighteen (by only two weeks) the punitive measure mandated was a two-week session on the topic of alcoholism. The program had no effect on me; I remained in a state of ignorance concerning the disease for the next twenty-five years.

Despite the seriousness of my actions, my parents allowed me to follow through with the plans I had made to go to Florida with one of my friends for spring break. Our itinerary started with traveling to Naples on a Greyhound bus, then spending the week with her aunt and uncle. Being given the nod to traverse unchaperoned over a thousand miles from home surprised me, especially after just being arrested.

It bewildered me as much as another incident that contained an illegal substance: when my dad found a quarter-pound of Columbian buds in my purse, he gave it back to me. Pleading with him it would cost me sixty dollars if he threw it away, I lied and said it wasn't mine; I was holding it for a schoolmate. He told me he would return it to me on one condition: the person who bought it would pick it up the next day. I agreed, so he placed the marijuana in a tool drawer in the kitchen. The following morning, after he left for work, I took the pot to school and quickly sold three ounces for twenty dollars each, keeping the fourth for myself. When my dad came home from work that evening, he asked if I completed the transaction, to which I replied yes. What a tangled web of lies I was weaving.

~~~~~~~~

The more I anesthetized myself, the darker my life became. I was no longer the extroverted little girl who came into the world all smiles and happy to be alive. After Michael died, I donned masks to protect myself. I ceased to grow into the young person who could one day exclaim, "The world is my oyster," and morphed into the person I thought others wanted me to be, pretending to be someone I was not.

The assaults from three years before still left me vulnerable and broken, and I shrouded myself in a cloak of darkness. The more repressed my emotions became, the further into a vortex I was sucked with such force, I couldn't climb out. I was living under a shadow where no light shined, save one tiny glimmer. It whispered in a subtle tone, urging me to rise each morning and face the day.

Thinking this must be my soul speaking, that spiritual part of my human existence where God resides, provided me enough courage not to end my life. Although my heart was laden with great losses, I knew in my core God was there. With this faith and conviction, as well as by acting *as if*, I managed to complete high school.

Throughout my years growing up, my parents never talked about feelings. Although I know they loved me, there was a disconnect when conveying emotions. I'm sure it had to do with their upbringing and lack of intimacy. You didn't say, "I love you," back then. My parents also afforded my brother and I with too much freedom, coupled with a lack of discipline. I remember my dad saying he would see to it that his children never had to go through what he did, meaning the absence of material comforts, as well as a strict upbringing with chores.

It was expected that I would attend college. For that reason, I chose to enroll in all college prep courses, such as chemistry, physics, and trigonometry. Feeling the need to please my parents and not myself, I didn't even consider artistic classes, which would deepen my creativity. Besides, I came from the "look-good" family, where everything looked good on the outside. Little did anyone know, I was slowly and painfully dying on the inside.

Just when I thought my emotional state couldn't get any worse, it did, when I was seventeen. Living on the edge was normal for me, so when I met a much older man at a party and later accepted a dinner date with him, I didn't think much of it. When we got to Roger's home and another man was there, a gnawing in my gut began to churn, and I could feel my hair stand on end. The situation just didn't feel right; why was this other person there? As I felt something ominous was about to occur, the fight-or-flight response familiar to me began to stir.

Dinner was over, and Roger's friend sat back in a recliner and appeared to pass out in a flash. As if on cue, he began to assault me. With one hand firmly gripping my throat, he pressed hard against my hyoid bone, making breathing difficult for me. Roger unzipped my jeans with his other hand and proceeded to violently rape me.

Terrified to fight back for fear of being strangled, I let go of any struggle and began to feel weightless. During the assault, I had an out-of-body experience that allowed me to escape the trauma as it was occurring. It was as if I were an observer, looking down at the crime occurring, and not the victim herself.

After it was over, the weight of Roger's body pressed heavily into mine, for what seemed like hours. Time ticked by in slow motion as the reality of the situation settled into my psyche. Not sure if he would inflict further harm, I fought back the tears, acting like everything was normal as I discreetly got dressed.

I became numb, desensitized of feeling again. The pattern, so ingrained, felt like second nature to me. Even though Roger's friend was a coward, never lifting a finger to help me throughout the attack, he later apologized for not coming to my aid. He too was intimidated by this evil man and his deviant behavior.

The violent assault led to further detachment, allowing me to compartmentalize the guilt, shame, and self-loathing I had for myself. The only coping mechanisms that were available to me now were maladaptive: self-blame, where I internalized the problem and blamed myself for it, and denial, where I denied the issue, maintaining it through alcohol and drugs.

By this time, I was a regular binge drinker, on the fast track to becoming a blackout drinker, where I would perform activities such as driving a car but had total lack of memory the next day, or experience even darker consequences, such as going home with and waking up next to complete strangers. Spinning out of control, I sunk deeper into that dark crevice, into the abyss.

CHAPTER 5

Struck by Lightning

Thunder is good, thunder is impressive,
but it's lightning that does the work.

~ Mark Twain ~

Graduation day was here. It was June 6, 1976 (ironically, this was the same day I got sober, twenty-four years later). The University of Delaware, located thirty minutes south in Newark, accepted my application, and I was excited to move out of my parents' house and be on my own for the very first time. At the same time, I was entering a phase of life that would challenge my decision-making to the hilt.

Freshman year was uneventful in the grand scheme of things. My drinking continued, made more accessible by taking quick trips down to Elkton, Maryland, where the legal age to purchase alcohol was eighteen. The dorm I lived in, Rodney, was in a quad, and on weekends, when parties were in high gear, a few brave students would streak through the square. Being a comedian, I eagerly placed one of my stereo speakers out the window as I cranked up "Mr. Skin" from Spirit's LP, *The Twelve Dreams of Dr. Sardonicus.*

One other noteworthy event I can recall is when I attended a party at Christiana Towers. Without warning, a premonition flashed through my mind that someone stole my Raleigh Grand Prix ten-speed. I told one of my friends, "I have to go. Someone stole my bike." When I arrived at the spot I had locked it up, sure enough, it was missing. At that moment, I don't remember what was more incredible: the act of thievery itself, or my intuition that told me so. The self-destruction I inflicted upon myself in the years to come was partially caused by not heeding this intuitive side.

Spring break arrived in early April, and my mother had driven down to pick me up and take me home for the week. Little did she know I had a surprise for her. When she came up to my room, I asked, "Guess what?" There was a quizzical look on her face, and before she could say anything, I bellowed out, "I'm going to Myrtle Beach!"

Her demeanor still called for an explanation, so I enlightened her, saying it was a last-minute plan and three other dorm mates were going. They had rented a house with four bedrooms for a mere eighty dollars, thus costing each of us just twenty bucks. Since it was a once in a lifetime deal, my mother took me home to do my laundry and whisked me right back down to the university. With our suitcases packed, we were ready to set out on our excursion, but only after agreeing to be safe first.

Road trip. Woo hoo! Four young women let loose in the spring of 1977. We navigated our route the old-fashioned way: with a map. There were no cell phones or GPSs to guide us. A little over ten hours into the trip, we entered South Carolina and began to be on the lookout for a liquor store. We couldn't locate one to save our lives, and the Addict in me began to become anxious; the craving for alcohol was increasing by the hour.

It wasn't until we stopped for gas and asked the attendant that we discovered the liquor stores in South Carolina had no signposts and were identifiable only by red dots painted on the buildings. Having passed dozens of buildings with red dots, we felt like boneheads. Once we procured our liquor, we drove to our beach house, isolated on an island, by crossing the only bridge that connected it to the mainland.

After fixing ourselves strong drinks, we were itching to go out on the town for the night after our exhausting journey, so without unpacking, we threw our suitcases on the beds and left. Walking down the strip, we inspected the numerous clubs, finally agreeing on one in particular. Inside, we encountered two young men, and after several rounds of drinks, we decided it would be a wild and crazy idea to kidnap them back to our place. They would be at our mercy.

The booze flowed nonstop throughout the night; I had no recollection of what occurred, only that when I came to, one of our hostages was lying naked next to me. I had just experienced my first blackout and had no idea what happened or who the other person was. The Addict's grip was becoming stronger, as I was entering the middle stage of alcoholism, characterized by craving, loss of control, and blackouts.

Before I could move, I heard noises coming from the kitchen. I gingerly got out of bed, grabbed my robe, and headed to investigate what I now realized was the clinking of glasses. Suddenly, there was a booming voice saying something about the hair of the dog, and everyone rushed in to see the other captive mixing vodka with OJ. In order to quell the throbbing in my head, I joined them in drinking screwdrivers for breakfast.

The Addict's shadow thoroughly enjoyed the powerlessness it was creating. My behavior would stir up untold messes with chaotic consequences, and since the shadow Addict does not like order, it will go to great lengths to disrupt it.

Despite the intervals where there was a loss of control and a lack of memory or blackouts, the four of us enjoyed a fantastic spring break. The drive home was as long as it was tiresome, but we arrived safe, much to the relief of our parents.

The remainder of the semester was uneventful, and before I knew it, summer was here. Each passing day, the Addict archetype dug its heels in deeper and deeper into my innermost self, tightening its grip in an extremely furtive manner.

My dad was a bigwig at National Vulcanized Fibre (NVF), a fiberglass manufacturer with several local plants, and he secured a summer job for me at the Wilmington plant. I earned $7.50 an hour in 1977, which was unprecedented, considering the minimum wage was only $2.30. The work was demanding, as there was no air-conditioning, but I reveled in the thought of the hefty sum that awaited me at summer's end. I would take that pot of gold with me in the fall when I returned to the University of Delaware.

Sophomore year found me residing in Christiana Towers, a high-rise dorm housing up to four students per room. It was the place to be, especially in the age of disco, where there was plenty of room to dance and, of course, party. And party we did. Kegs of beer were the norm on weekends and the occasional Thursday night. In truth, if you didn't reserve one several days ahead, you were simply out of luck because the U of D was one of the East Coast's biggest party schools.

On Sunday, February 5, 1978, a snowstorm began to form, and the snow continued to fall Monday morning as I prepared to go to my eight o'clock class. No one was aware of the phenomenon we were experiencing: thundersnow, the unusual combination of thunder, lightning, and snow. According to *Scientific American*, thundersnow is unique, because due to subzero temperatures, interactions between supercooled liquid water, ice crystals, and larger ice particles also generate lightning.

They further state that by the time the lightning flashes during a storm like this, it is often already too late to notify residents.

Not knowing the magnitude and danger of the storm, I proceeded to trek the long walk to early classes, along with the other students. The snow was falling at such a substantial rate, it was challenging to see let alone navigate through it. Walking home was no different, so I popped open my umbrella to help keep the continuous pummel of snowflakes from stinging my eyes.

As I approached the Towers and passed the tennis courts, surrounded by twelve-foot chain link fences, I was paralyzed by a pink flash in the sky. Before I could react, my only thought was, *I'm dead.* In an instant, several images of my life as a child slowly entered my stream of consciousness. I experienced a searing pain as the lightning bolt's electrical discharge traveled down the umbrella and up through my right arm.

Am I dying? I wondered. *Is this it? No, this can't be happening; I don't want to die yet.*

The discharge knocked me unconscious, and when I opened my eyes, I found myself lying on my back with six pairs of eyes peering down at me. I heard someone ask, "Are you hurt? Are you okay?" A couple of the students said they saw the lightning strike the umbrella and hurl me several feet in the air before I landed on my back. I let out a huge sigh of relief, uttering the words, "Thank you, God, I'm alive."

Intense tingling and numbness surged in my right arm, and although it felt like it was asleep, it was painful. Sitting up cautiously, I took several deep breaths. I was still stunned at the fact lightning just struck me, and I survived. With assistance, I stood on my feet and walked to the dorm, where I proceeded to call my mother.

I related my harrowing experience; my mother was very concerned, giving me instructions to go to the hospital for an examination.

"Sure thing," I said and then did what any college student with a major alcohol problem would do: I went to my room, drank a six-pack of beer, and passed out. A lightning strike would not deter the Addict one bit. In fact, even more energy emanated, and its power would only increase its hold on me.

My right arm and hand had the sensation of painful spasms, while still feeling numb, for several days. That, however, seemed to be the only side effect of the lightning strike. Unknown to me at the time, the next thirty years would give birth to many unexplained physical ailments and pain. This lack of awareness added to the dark cloud hovering over me, choking out what tiny light was left inside.

Three months after the lightning strike, I felt a sudden surge that caused me to become dizzy and a bit disoriented. It only lasted a second or two, but the effect was startling. My eyes seemed to be crossing involuntarily; I couldn't prevent the spasms from occurring. After a number of incidents, my mother was concerned enough to schedule an appointment for me with her ophthalmologist.

After a thorough examination, he pronounced my eyes as perfect, with no irregularities. Since I had no further issues with the lightning strike, I failed to mention it. Because I put the incident in the back of my mind, the eventual diagnosis of convergent spasms, where the electrical impulses misfire in the brain, was delayed.

The balance of my undergraduate years marked a definite increase in binge drinking, as well as blackouts for me. One notable exception was the fall semester in 1979, when I lived at home and made dean's list; this was easily explained by the fact that living under my parents' roof curtailed my drinking.

The Student archetype, which suggests a pattern of constant learning, was in an intense battle with the shadow side of the Addict, which represents a struggle with willpower and the absence of self-control. The Addict was successful in all cases, save for this one.

Having an insatiable thirst for knowledge and the desire to master new subjects, I chose courses that were challenging and not the standard undergraduate electives. I gravitated toward the sciences and opted to enroll in astronomy, human heredity and genetics, and chemistry. It was my final semester at the University of Delaware, the spring of 1980, when I chose the latter course, which caused my friends to deem me insane. They didn't know how powerful the Student archetype had developed within me, nor the conflict it presented with the Addict.

There were two incidents I can recall where my drinking caused grave consequences. They both occurred my senior year; one was in the fall, and the other in the spring of 1980. The first episode where alcohol played a detrimental role in my life was when a Newark policeman arrested me for walking along the highway while intoxicated. Fortunately (or not), I had lost my car keys, as they had somehow fallen into a storm drain. The officer saw me, stopped his patrol car, and got out to question me. After smelling alcohol on my breath, he handcuffed me, and for the second time in my young life, I was wearing a set of matching silver bracelets.

Sitting in the back of the patrol car, I was conniving ways to get out of this situation; I did not want to spend the night in jail. My only choice was to call my dad, and with another bout of alcohol-fueled disgrace and remorse, I revealed what happened. Once again, he came to the rescue, bailing me out. As I look through the rearview mirror, I realize he should have let me spend the night in jail, where I would have had the time to contemplate the consequences of my actions.

The second occasion occurred the night before an economics midterm, when I got drunk and passed out. By the time I came to, the class and the exam had ended. I knew I would fail the course by missing it, so I called the professor and explained I was too sick to get out of bed and pleaded to take a makeup exam. He obliged and gave me the information for the retest. Making sure I was on time *and* prepared, I took the midterm and passed the course. Another narrow escape.

My college years were tainted with the Scarlet Letter, and although the letter was still an A, this time it stood for Alcohol. I was unable to comprehend the choke hold it had on me, nor realize it was only going to get worse. There were countless times I placed myself in dangerous and potentially life-threatening situations, and only by the grace of God did I survive. Denial ain't a river in Egypt.

After graduation, I began to have severe headaches that were so intense it felt like a hammer was banging on my head. Desperate for relief, I made appointments with every doctor who treated migraines but found no answers. They continued with such magnitude I was referred to the Jefferson Headache Clinic in Philadelphia to see if they could diagnose the problem.

After multiple tests, including a CAT scan and an MRI, they could find no cause. Eventually, after over two years and numerous medications, they dissipated. Ultimately, it would be discovered that the lightning strike contributed migraines to the list of my unexplained pain and medical issues, including the interval ten years later where the spasms interrupted my daily life and activities.

Little did I know, migraines would be the least of my worries.

CHAPTER 6

Allergic to Alcohol

If you are allergic to alcohol ... can you take shots for that?
~ Shmuel Breban ~

I am allergic to alcohol. I break out in spots: New York, Philadelphia, Washington DC. In fact, it was the summer of 1980, and I had just graduated with a bachelor's degree in business, when I broke out in the spot of New York City after an invitation for a weekend getaway by a friend who worked in the entertainment industry.

Elizabeth was invited to an exclusive party and imagined it would be an exciting event for the two of us to attend while spending a few days together. Since anything with the word *party* attached to it was on my To-Do list, the idea was enticing. With that thought in mind, I packed a bag and made the two-hour drive to her apartment, arriving late that night.

We relaxed for the better part of the next day, knowing we would be up until the early hours of the morning. As we readied ourselves, putting on the finishing touches of our makeup, I felt like a teenager about to go on her first date: excited, but nervous too. Elizabeth was tall, beautiful, and blonde, with striking facial features, high cheekbones, and dark-blue eyes. She was everything I was not.

Alcohol changed that, however; it transformed me, bringing out my Femme Fatale archetype, which used my beauty and sexuality to manipulate men. It was the oil that lubricated the squeaky wheel. On one side of the coin, a few drinks allowed me to feel smarter, prettier, and funnier, but on the other hand, it lowered my inhibitions, changing me into Mrs. Hyde, who engaged in aberrant behavior, illustrating its shadow aspects.

We left the apartment after downing a couple of drinks to loosen up. Arriving at the venue, its sheer size surprised me. It was as grand as Studio 54 in its heyday. As I surveyed the area, watching the throng of people jockeying for the best position in line to get in, I felt like a tiny drop of water in the vast, expansive ocean, outnumbered and insignificant. I needed an about-face, so as soon as we went in, I immediately hightailed it to the bar and ordered a Tanqueray and bitter lemon with a twist of lime.

After a few dances and drinks, I found myself alone in another sea of humanity. Elizabeth was nowhere in sight, but instead of searching for her, I ordered another drink. That was the last thing I remember before I fell into one of my blackouts, that were now occurring more frequently.

The next thing I remember was hearing a knock on a door; I appeared to be in a luxurious hotel suite. Room service entered, wheeling in a cart with a bottle of Dom Perignon, champagne flutes, and a bowl of strawberries with fresh whipped cream. The warm, muscular body lying next to me sat up and thanked the server. *Who was this gorgeous man? How did I get here? Most importantly, where was I?*

While I'll never know the answer to the first two questions, as well as many more that followed, I do know I was a guest of the famous Waldorf Astoria. *At least I'm a high-class drunk*, I thought, downplaying my problem drinking.

Another typical scenario unfolded one morning a few months later, when, as my eyes began to open and adjust to the bright sunlight that filtered through unfamiliar window blinds, a concrete skyscraper was center stage. That queasy churning in my gut intensified as I began to shake off the cobwebs from the alcohol of the night before, realizing it happened again; I went home with someone, and I had no clue who it was or where I was.

Springing from the bed to the window, I parted the shades with my fingers and heard a nervous voice that was mine ask, "Where am I?"

Humiliation and remorse flooded my veins as I paused for the reply.

"Philly," a voice grunted.

I now had broken out in the spot of Philadelphia.

As if on autopilot, the next words I uttered were "How did I get here?" There was a quiet foreboding before I comprehended the words expressed by an unfamiliar voice: "You came with me."

I paused, just for an instant, allowing sarcasm to creep in. *Oh*, I thought, *this is a man of many words. Could he be more verbose?* But just as quickly as it crawled in, it was gone, clearing the way for the more familiar guilt and shame to take its place.

Feeling neither safe nor secure, I refrained from asking the question I was most curious about: *Who are you?* At this moment, my primary purpose was to return to my car without any further complications.

The contempt and loathing I held for myself heightened with each abject deed I perpetrated. The somber truth was, I was unable to make healthy decisions, and it was impossible for me to think I could control my behavior. I was powerless over alcohol, and my life *was* unmanageable.

Stinkin' thinkin' was rooted deep within my psyche, and several decades would pass before my mind was clear enough to make sound rational decisions. I had not yet hit my rock bottom.

My judgment was cloudy at best and downright reckless at worst, which was exhibited by my decision to go to Washington DC for a weekend getaway. After accepting the invitation from Bob, a friendly although portly acquaintance, I opted to travel by train to safeguard against a possible DWI/DUI arrest.

Bob was waiting at the station when my train pulled in and, after taking my overnight bag, ushered me to his hotel room so I could freshen up. There was not an ounce of chemistry running through my veins for him, which left me to feel hesitant and acutely uncomfortable.

Questioning my motivation for accepting his proposal, I realized the answer was because I wanted to elevate my self-esteem. Bob was prosperous, allowing him to buy the highest quality alcohol, and he ran in elite circles. Once more, it was another failed attempt, believing external situations could heal my inner wounds.

The Prostitute archetype, strengthened by the Femme Fatale's presence, reared its ugly head, and despite the fact I had no intention of sleeping with him, I led him to believe so. The Femme Fatale, the seductress of society, reverses the power roles of men by dominating them with their looks and sexuality. They are drawn to seducing men with money and power, and this archetype had been maturing alongside of me for some time.

Even in an alcohol-induced fog, I had to draw a line somewhere, as the thought of having sex with an overweight man repulsed me; being critical of obesity was rooted in my psyche.

However, I had no inkling of how the evening would unfold nor how I would avoid a liaison with him.

We dressed for dinner and made our way to one of the most exclusive restaurants in the district. Bob was a lifelong friend of the owner and paid to have the top floor shut down, so we could dine in private. Thinking I should be treated this way all the time, I felt a keen sense of entitlement, judging myself as deserving this lifestyle.

Two service attendants hovered over us, filling our water glasses, while emptying our ashtrays, ensuring our needs were met. We placed our order, and thankfully, small talk ensued. Before long, the head waiter returned with our appetizer: escargots à la Bourguignonne.

Having never sampled this delicacy before, I cautiously nibbled on one end. Salty, I mused and proceeded to eat the entire hors d'oeuvre, a faux pas on my behalf because I needed to swallow a healthy swig of my Tanqueray to keep it down.

A solo pianist began to perform melodious tunes that buoyed our spirits, at least temporarily, as we finished our meal. Sipping on Courvoisier, we sat back and enjoyed the relaxing music. The liquor filled my veins with a warm sensation while lowering my inhibitions. The unbridled force was nearing the light, and I was powerless to stop it.

After we drank our second cognac, the piano man took a break, giving Bob an implicit indication to introduce cocaine to the evening. He poured a substantial amount on the Steinway piano and divided the white powder into long lines, using his platinum credit card. He pulled a Benjamin Franklin out of his pocket, rolled it into a straw, and handed it to me.

As I snorted the cocaine, the burning in my nostril subsided as the numbing effects quickly materialized, and so the onset of an obsessive cycle began to emerge: the more alcohol consumed, the more cocaine snorted. It was a vicious whirlwind propelling me into inappropriate behavior, such as climbing onto the piano and doing push-ups. It was time for us to leave.

Strolling down the street, we passed a popular nightclub and agreed to have a nightcap. It was vital for me to find a way of escape from Bob. I decided it was best for me to hook up with someone else, and I proceeded to scan the bar for a suitable and attractive partner. After finishing our nightcap, Bob stated it was time to leave.

Not wanting to return with him to his room, I replied I would be there shortly. The next memory I have is coming to in a strange hotel room with a strange man. Washington DC was now the third spot where I broke out. I looked at the clock and shouted, "Holy shit, I missed my train!"

Topping it off, Bob left, leaving me stranded without my belongings. How was I to get home, and more importantly, what would happen with my job?

My drinking was making my life unmanageable, giving rise to complete and utter chaos. A moment of hesitation invaded my consciousness, but I swiftly pushed it aside; for the umpteenth time, I knew I had to call my father to bail me out. Although I arrived home late and missed a day of work, I didn't get fired — yet. There were always more yets to come.

My binge drinking was out of control, and I was on a collision course with every negative outcome possible. This was evident by not one but two incidents that took place throughout the next, most volatile stage of my drinking. I can only surmise God had a veil of protection over me during this time, which I consider being one of the dark nights of my soul.

No physical harm befell me as a by-product of the erratic and irresponsible choices I made while under the influence of alcohol. It is as judicious to prevent an intoxicated person from driving as it is irresponsible for an inebriated person to get behind the wheel of a car. But on one evening in January 1982, my thinking wasn't rational after consuming half a bottle of Tanqueray at my boss's party, and I declined my friend's offer to drive me home.

My combativeness and insanity were quite apparent; if anyone were going to get into an accident in my car, it would be me. Only minutes after driving down the road, red and blue lights were flashing behind us, along with a blaring siren. *Uh-oh. What did I do now?*

The policeman approached my window and asked me if I was aware of why he stopped me. Naturally, not only was I oblivious that I was going 20 mph *under* the speed limit, but I was also driving down the wrong side of the street. He asked me to take a Breathalyzer test, and I refused, ignorant that not complying resulted in the automatic loss of my license.

After I was ordered out of the car and placed in a set of shiny handcuffs for the third time, the officer asked my friend if he was sober enough to drive my car, and he acknowledged he was. At the police station, I placed a phone call to my brother, who was back home for an extended visit. He was irritated by the intrusion but reluctantly bailed me out. For me, I went on with life as normal, or as normal as a raging alcoholic's chaotic life can be.

Several months passed, and then, without warning, there it was: a letter from the state of Delaware notifying me that they were revoking my driver's license. My brother, who just happened to get the mail that day, intercepted it and informed my parents of its contents. When confronted, the usual wave of guilt and shame washed over me; I was a worthless loser, a derelict. I wasn't able to see the truth: it wasn't *me* doing these horrible things, it was the Addict in me that was causing me to make the decisions that led me away from the straight and narrow.

But for the grace of God, once more, I escaped with a lenient penalty for my unlawful actions: a seventy-five-dollar fine, mandatory attendance in an Alcohol Awareness class for four weeks (which I called "Wino College"), and a provisional license to and from work for three months. A lack of severity in the consequences for my immoral, and sometimes illegal, actions prevented me from putting the plug in the jug and confronting my demons head on.

The following year, not even the most harrowing and, by far, most terrifying experience could bring me to my knees. The night was late when I entered the Brandywine Club, my usual after-hours establishment. Despite being previously flagged by Jack, the bouncer, for passing out on the piano bar, I somehow found myself in his car as we drove through the back roads of Brandywine Valley.

As he was driving, Jack's hand began to stroke my thigh. I pushed it away, rejecting his solicitation. Undeterred, he kept trying, and each time I rebuffed him. Finally incensed by my rejection, he violently and forcefully pushed me out of the car into the freezing night. Before I realized what happened, I caught a glimpse of fading red taillights disappearing into the darkness.

Fear planted a massive stranglehold on me, its grip so tight I had to fight for my breath. After a few paralyzing moments, and what seemed like an eternity, I knew if I were to survive, it was imperative to get help. My dilemma, however, was twofold: I had no idea where I was, and more significant, I was highly intoxicated.

As I sat and began to get a feel for my surroundings, I noticed it was pitch-black, save for a random twinkling star peeking through the trees and thicket that lined the steep hills. Scrutinizing every angle, I caught the glimmer of a single light situated far up on a hill. It was barely visible, but shining it was. I summoned all my courage and took several deep breaths, watching the condensation form with each exhale. The will to live outweighed any alarms that rang within me; it was crucial I reach the glow that called out to me.

Still feeling unbalanced, I cautiously began to stand and felt the heel of my Aigner pumps wobble on the uneven, frozen soil. Placing one foot in front of the other, I was determined to forge ahead, clearing the vines and brush out the way. The terrain was hazardous: I tripped over a rock and fell, breaking off the heel of one of my shoes. Getting back on my feet was a challenge, as it would be for any inebriated woman in stilettos, attempting to climb rocky terrain at three o'clock in the morning.

Against the odds, I reached the front door, exhausted, short of breath, and frozen, but full of gratitude. I continually rang the doorbell until a woman answered. Somehow, someway, I managed to communicate my predicament and gave my father's phone number to her. I waited outside, trembling, while she placed the call to give him directions to her house.

The interval, which felt like an eternity, was just forty minutes. The headlights of my dad's car beamed as he drove up the sharp incline to the house. After mumbling a teary-eyed thank you, I staggered over to the car and got in. Neither my father nor I spoke a single word the entire ride home; the silence was deafening.

Once again, like a boomerang, remorse and humiliation festered within me, like a cesspool on a hot, humid day. When was enough, enough? The condition I was in needed immediate attention. My life depended on it. How much lower would I get before I offered my hand? The answer, thank God, was less than one week away.

CHAPTER 7

Putting Down the Drink

I can't convince you to put the drink down if you're an alcoholic, you have to want to do that.... And that takes responsibility.

~ Don Young ~

The first position I held after graduating from college was as a key manager assistant (KMA), overseeing seven hard-line departments for the discount retailer Jefferson Ward. It was during this tumultuous time when I was arrested and missed several days of work. The period between my drinking binges narrowed, placing my career in jeopardy, particularly when I came into work with alcohol on my breath. Management occasionally sent me home, and I was phased out of my position after two years.

On a positive note, being fired allowed me to file for unemployment benefits. It was the summer of 1982, when Jeff, my boyfriend at the time, and I celebrated by taking a road trip to Myrtle Beach. Deja vu, all over again. But reality soon set in, and by September, I began to search for new employment.

Finding an ad in the local paper for an outside sales rep in office supplies, I applied for the job and got it. The company trained me as the first EZ Order girl, complete with a tabletop flip chart. By now, my drinking became a daily habit, and I would go to the basement, with rum and Coke in hand, and set my appointments for the week.

It continued to be my daily practice until one day in January I faced a stunning proposal that left me resolute and unwavering. It was January 9, 1983, and for me, a day that will live in infamy. Still a fledgling in the nest, I enjoyed watching the NFL playoffs with my dad and a cold beer. When I went to the refrigerator for a Heineken, I asked if he wanted one too. His response caught me off-guard, stopping me dead in my tracks.

My dad offered me a challenge. He said, "If you quit drinking from today until Easter, which is April 3, I will give you $1,000."

Excuse me; did I hear you correctly? You'll give me $1,000 to stop my alcohol consumption for a mere three months? Dollar signs, huge dollar signs, appeared in my mind. I could feel the wheels begin to turn in my head; money was a motivating factor in my life, merely for the fact I didn't have any.

Before I could consider any argument against it, I readily agreed to the challenge. The lack of willpower, one of the shadow aspects of the Addict, along with the Victim's and the Artist's shadows, were in store for a battle royal. The issue, I would identify twenty years later, was that I had no internal measuring device to balance this power.

Although someone could look at me and say I was in the light aspect of the Addict for giving up the hold alcohol had on me, I was not. Only my external strength was evident, not my inner spirit. I became what is known as a dry drunk, and that's how I lived for the next seventeen years, extending the image of looking good on the outside, yet slowly dying on the inside.

For the remainder of the day, I encountered little to no physical distress as a result of the withdrawal of alcohol. Later that evening when I tried to fall asleep and couldn't, I began to regret my decision. My alcoholism was extensive enough to cause annoying twitches and spasms, which prevented me from sleeping. They continued for the better part of a week until finally, slumber came.

The next month, I moved into an apartment with my boyfriend; my parents were apprehensive but could say little; I would be twenty-five in April. There was added concern for them when they learned we went to a bar, and I ordered a double: a double 7-Up, with a cherry. Respecting my decision not to drink, Jeff asked for a Coke, as he felt it better not to drink around me. I appreciated the gesture, but we *were* in a bar surrounded by people consuming alcohol.

Easter came and went, and I met the three-months challenge. My father had financial issues at the time, though, so he was only able to offer me $400 of the original amount. I could have been disappointed about the money, but I wasn't. Instead, I was grateful my life was healthier than it was before. For one thing, I was not coming to in places I didn't belong—alcoholics don't wake up, they come to. For another, I wasn't getting arrested or hadn't lost my job.

As I continued down the path of abstinence, the thought of using alcohol to celebrate New Year's Eve constantly remained in the forefront of my mind. However, the holiday came and went without it. By now, I felt I had cleaned up my act and straightened out my life.

When it was suggested I attend an AA meeting, I took exception, objecting that I wasn't an alcoholic, just someone who, after two drinks, found it difficult to replace my drink with a non-alcoholic one. I eventually did attend a meeting and left feeling justified about not going. Everyone who spoke was miserable, complaining about not being able to drink, while I, on the other hand, was ecstatic.

We were not on the same page; I compared myself out, as I looked only at the differences we had and not the similarities we shared. I suffered from a form of terminal uniqueness; I wasn't like those people. Years later, when sober, I realized I was a dry drunk, the term Father Bill uses when the only thing an alcoholic does is put down the drink; they don't change. My life got better, but I didn't. AA tells you your life might not get better; you may lose your job, your house, or even your spouse, but you will get better.

Although I didn't drink alcohol, the Addict's shadow was not only prevalent and in control but very active. After two years, I ended my relationship with Jeff because of his addiction to heroin, a drug I feared intensely, and his dishonesty. The Addict had me in a headlock. I was calling the kettle black — I was using methamphetamine, a drug called crank on the streets, a less potent, though just as dangerous, form of crystal meth.

Snorting was the usual method to ingest the drug, but a deviated septum prevented me from doing this, so I opened any analgesic in capsule form and poured out its contents. I then filled the empty container it with crank, which, at times was in a semi-liquid form. It was my little *happy pill* because, for the next twelve hours, it gave me the energy to clean my house, organize, and make phone calls.

Being under the influence of this drug not only strained the relationships within my family, but it also curbed my appetite, causing me to lose significant weight. At my lowest, I was 105 pounds and extremely thin. The *ism* in alcoholism blocked my entire awareness for a healthy lifestyle, and as a result, I increasingly craved more of the drug. Maybe that is why it's called alcohol-ism and not alcohol-wasm.

Life went on with its ups and mostly downs, but there were occasional moments when the shroud of darkness dissipated. One case in point occurred the following year, when a new career opportunity, with the potential for a substantial increase in income, presented itself: an outside sales position with an epoxy flooring company that was a leader in the industry.

When my father, an industrial engineer for National Vulcanized Fibre, complained to a manager that he was always late for their meetings, he was told the reason was because they were shorthanded. Shortly after that, my dad mentioned that I was in outside sales, and they told him to have me call for an interview. I did and was offered the job.

The following fall, in 1984, Donnie, my brother, who graduated from the Southwestern University of Law in LA the day after I graduated from the U of D, was studying for the Delaware Bar Exam. He intended to practice corporate law in Delaware in view of its lenient tax laws and the substantial number of companies incorporated here.

While he was reviewing for the exam, he worked part-time selling life insurance and annuities. Donnie didn't have life insurance, since he just quit smoking cigarettes and wanted to wait for the one-year mark to lower his premium. During the third week of October, he had a constant fever and was lethargic, so my mother suggested he make a doctor's appointment.

After a thorough examination, the doctor ordered blood work to confirm a diagnosis and called to have him come into his office the next day. When they returned home, I received a phone call from my father, evoking a tragic memory that laid dormant for twenty years. As he spoke, the words echoed in my ear, and my world was rocked once more, changing it forever: "Debbie," he said, his voice quivering, "Donnie has leukemia."

Immediately carried back to the day I received the phone call at my Aunt Dot's, I felt my body become just as tense. I felt the pain of my breaking heart and the tears on my cheeks. And more significantly, I felt the denial. Oh, the denial. *This can't be happening again*, I thought, as my anger and bitterness at God increased by the second.

But it was, and as I sat down on the sofa I was cleaning, holding the phone in one hand and the vacuum in the other, grief and outrage squeezed my soul so hard a fire ignited that would serve me for the following four years of his illness.

My brother was diagnosed with chronic myelogenous leukemia, or CML. Although this type of leukemia was rare in someone as young as my brother, I was determined to help him fight it by learning everything I could about the disease. Having the Student archetype was, in many ways, a blessing in my life. However, none of the information I acquired could release him from his eventual death sentence.

Donnie's twenty-eighth birthday fell during the ten days he was hospitalized to begin his initial treatment. CML is mainly caused by the Philadelphia chromosome, an abnormality of chromosome 22, where it is shortened because of an exchange, or translocation, between chromosomes 22 and 9 during cell division. This translocation takes place in a single bone marrow cell, which in turn produces more of these mutant cells.

There are three phases to this type of leukemia. The first phase is the chronic phase, where most people are diagnosed, and where there is an increased number of white blood cells. The second stage is the accelerated one, where there is a high white blood cell count, and the CML cells are growing faster, causing fatigue, fever, and weight loss. The final phase is the blast crisis, where there is a very high white blood cell count, and the CML cells have new chromosome abnormalities and spread to the bone marrow and other organs. The symptoms here are severe. Regardless of the fact Donnie was in the chronic stage, he would require not only these ten days, but three full months of hospitalization, which began the following January.

The invoices for the first ten days totaled around $10,000, and the cost of the three-month stay was an overwhelming $150,000. Fortunately, my father went to his company and explained the situation, and NVF hired my brother and then fired him, all on paper. As a result, Blue Cross was authorized to disburse the necessary payment. Finding the courage to battle a terminal disease is strenuous enough, let alone having the financial burden looming over your head. And so his journey began.

While Donnie was fighting an incurable illness, I was wrestling with my own internal conflict arising from opposing impulses. Again and again, I would repeat patterns of behavior, ending with the same adverse outcome. Most of these were relationship oriented, but the Addict in me was so potent, I became irritated by the oscillation of my goals and actions: wanting to save money, yet spending frivolously, wanting to gain weight, yet binging and later purging.

The rationale behind this conduct, Caroline Myss writes, is that the shadow (in my case, the shadow of the Addict) expresses itself through behavior that sabotages ourselves because we fear becoming empowered. She continues to say this leads to a painful conflict when we feel one way and act another, separating our heart, the fourth chakra, and our mind, the sixth chakra.

Chakras are storehouses of energy that transmit energy through spinning wheels, or vortexes, that are positioned throughout your body, from the base of your spine to the crown of your head. There are seven main chakras, each one corresponding to a different group of emotions, behaviors, physical organs, colors, and specific locations in the body. When a chakra system is balanced, we are in balance. Imbalanced chakras are related to psychological issues that, if left untreated, can lead to physical disease.

When your heart and mind are incongruent, or imbalanced, you *always* make unwise choices, which is your fifth chakra (throat or center of communication). The discrepancy between my experiences (choosing emotionally unavailable men, spending money) and awareness (choosing men who didn't need fixing, saving money) took its toll on me for the next thirteen distressing years.

I was in store for a major headache.

CHAPTER 8

Banging My Head against a Brick Wall

The important thing is to learn a lesson every time you lose. Life is a learning process, and you have to try to learn what's best for you. Let me tell you, life is not fun when you're banging your head against a brick wall all the time.

~ John McEnroe ~

Under the illusion that just by putting down the drink, everything in my life would snap back to normal, I didn't understand why I was happy about life in the physical world but still miserable within. When people shared at the only AA meeting I attended, I heard them complain about how tough it was to get through one hour without drinking, let alone one day.

For me, it was easy to get through the day; adverse effects were almost nonexistent because I didn't have drinking sprees or blackouts anymore. Life—work—was moving in a positive direction for the first time since I could remember. My new job paid extremely well; I received a 20 percent commission on every floor I sold. And one spring day in 1985, a significant milestone occurred, proving my success: I submitted a $125,000 purchase order to install an epoxy floor in the magnetic cell room for a local chemical company.

Working persistently for over nine months, the reward was one of the most exhilarating moments in my lifetime: a $25,000 commission. It was by far the most impressive result in my career. Calculating the amount of my compensation using today's inflation rate, it would be an astounding $56,155, making my achievement a peak, although brief, experience.

Despite attaining monetary success, I was haunted by several prejudicial occurrences of gender bias. The most egregious incident took place just prior to the installation of that magnetic cell room floor. Due to the many hazardous chemicals, including mercury, contained in the room, we all had to view a ninety-minute safety and training video.

The six men in my crew, as well as myself, sat patiently as the important, yet mundane, technical jargon and procedures were explained. Without warning, the scene deviated to a backyard with an in-ground pool, where you saw a person swimming under water. As they neared the end of the pool, suddenly, a beautiful woman burst out of the water. She was topless, and her bare breasts were visible for everyone to see.

The safety director grinned broadly and joked, "We just wanted to make sure all you boys were awake."

His words appalled me. After recovering from that degrading scene, I felt a wave of fury and indignation flood over me that only deepened when no apology was offered.

It was a man's world, and I was a fly in the ointment. To be effective and flourish in this industry, you needed to be one of the good ol' boys, and clearly, I was not. In the mid-eighties, it was an aberration for a woman to sell epoxy floors, let alone run a construction crew to install them. I frequently faced speed bumps or hurdles to cross, which left me thinking, *Why am I establishing myself in this career?* I was extremely sensitive to these obstacles, as they triggered my need to be seen and heard, a flashback of the wounds from my Invisible Child.

Another incident tested my knowledge and expertise of the entire application of an epoxy floor (calculating the area, cove base, pitch, amount of product and labor); it came when speaking to the maintenance director of a prestigious college in Delaware County, Pennsylvania. As I was explaining how to pitch (slope) the kitchen floor to the drain, he abruptly turned and directed his response to a crew member standing at my side. The installer, brand new and untrained, didn't have the faintest idea what the supervisor was talking about.

Striving to maintain my composure during this dry-drunk phase of my life was virtually impossible; I was extremely hypersensitive and took everything personally. My irritation began to seethe as I uttered, with a huff, "Excuse me, but he's not trained in this area and doesn't know how to pitch a floor. I'm the person you need to discuss the details with."

Intentionally ignoring me, the engineer spoke directly to the crewman and continued to turn a blind eye to me. My irritation grew into anger, bubbling inside, like a pool of hot tar, ready to scald anything it touched. It took every ounce of strength I had to control my emotions and not have an outburst. Walking away from the meeting, I decided I didn't want the job, even if we won the bid for it.

Ultimately, I was unfairly let go from the company and later sued them for sexual discrimination. Taking only my father and uncle to represent me, instead of experienced counsel, I was blown out of the water by their high-priced attorneys. I was angry and frustrated, and had a hair-trigger temper. My faith in God was tested many times during this transitional time.

While my professional career teetered, giving me euphoric highs and miserable lows, my personal life followed suit. In the summer of 1985, I began an affair with an over-the-road truck driver whose CB handle was Sly Fox. We had a chance encounter on the airwaves when my mother and I were taking a day trip to Rehoboth Beach in Delaware. For some unknown reason, the antenna to my CB radio had broken, and he offered to fix it. Pulling over to meet in a parking lot just south of Dover, I handed him the antenna, and in a few minutes, Rainbow, my CB handle, was up and running once more.

I thanked him as we went on our way, but there was an energetic connection, a chemistry I could not explain. It started as a spark and began to smolder inside. My thoughts were consumed by this stranger, thinking how, or even if, I would see him again. Much to my surprise, the wait was short-lived, as the very next evening, I heard a shout: "How 'bout you, Rainbow ... are you out here? Sly Fox is looking for you."

My heart skipped a beat as I wondered if it could be him. I answered, "You got Rainbow here, Sly Fox. What's your 40?" He was on Rt. 202 returning with a load of cement. We didn't meet that evening but soon after became enmeshed in an adulterous relationship, one with more twists and turns than a labyrinth.

The affair was an additional substitute for alcohol, plus I was still using crank, and these actions would add to my living on the edge in chaos for the next decade. The Addict, now fixated on the intoxication of being in love, was so powerful, I was unable to control my emotions, even when faced with the fact they were being played with. Five months of passion ensued, where I never wanted time to end. It was all a fairy tale, and I was living in a dream state. And that was the problem; I found dreaming was better than waking up into reality.

My low-self-esteem, the absence of my mother's nurturing, along with growing up indoctrinated with "happily ever after" endings were all indications of my addiction to love. I displayed many of the signs: I dreamt of my wedding and the white picket fence, I was rarely single, I stayed in a relationship even though it was wrong, I couldn't bear being alone, and I felt the need to change the other person.

For the next year, I continued to endure the emotional game of yo-yo love that Fox was playing with me, even though I was with other men. He knew how to pull every string, sometimes prolonging the agony for months until he called and stopped by. Fox was a drug I couldn't and didn't want to let go of; the thought of living without him grossly outweighed the fact we lived the majority of our lives apart.

The relationship ended in betrayal, leaving me broken and feeling devalued. Always desperate in the quest for change, I fell short countless times, unable to find the key to unlock the power to do so. I immersed myself in self-help topics to uncover any measures that would help me in my search. Religion was the first arena I dove into, attempting to solve the puzzle. I studied a concordance to the Bible (a gift from my brother), read Norman Vincent Peale's *The Power for Living*, and became born again, but it all failed to enlighten me.

Examining the concordance, I diligently parsed every verse from the New Testament and interpreted it in a modern context. The result: I remained a stubborn, rude, and self-centered person, full of self-loathing, although I did gain a deeper understanding of what spirituality meant.

At this stage of my life, the shadow of the Seeker archetype was emerging as I drifted from one author's views of the truth to another. I had no idea what exactly I was looking for; I only knew it was something other than what I presently had. In Caroline

Myss's words, I truly was that lost soul, someone on an aimless journey without direction, ungrounded, and disconnected from goals and others.

A few of the books I began to comb through focused on self-improvement, such as Nathanial Brandon's *Self-Esteem* and M. Scott Peck's *The Road Less Traveled*. In no time at all, my shelves were overflowing with books whose authors offered a variety of steps, actions, methods, and ways to find your truth through self-love, wholeness, happiness, and self-respect: everything I lacked.

There was another struggle taking place; this time it was between the Seeker, who wanted to find the answer to my spiritual bankruptcy, and the Addict, who was holding onto my powerlessness. The two were at odds as I devoured the material before me, comprehending it in theory but unable to integrate it into my consciousness. The Addict was running circles around the Seeker, as the black hole still residing in the pit of my stomach overflowed with external substances, while saturated with everything other than feeling love for myself.

During the early months of 1987, I met Steve, a drummer in a jazz fusion band. My relationship with him, doomed from the start (I was incapable of forming an intimate, long-lasting relationship), was unlike others, in that we had a Christian foundation. We were both spiritual. However, when we read from the Bible, we stopped every now and then to snort a line of cocaine. To many, this would appear to be sacrilegious, but living in a world of addiction, we felt (erroneous or not) a deeper connection with God.

Throughout our courtship, I noticed my inability to express my feelings, as well as how quickly I was to lose patience and get angry. Reflecting upon why I could not articulate my sentiments to Steve, I recognized I was afraid of being rejected again. When I felt my needs not being met, I reacted and lashed out, saying I was done with the relationship. For me, depending on a man was unthinkable because the thought of being rejected or abandoned was too painful. Additionally, there was the ingrained message from my father to never depend on a man.

Relationships such as this one held major space in the emptiness inside, living rent-free, and they were an enigma for me, as I explored far more than I would have liked. Something was amiss, and for the life of me, I was unable to figure it out. The Addict was cunning and powerful, and seemed to surface at unsuspecting times, like the whack-a-mole game on the boardwalk. Just when I thought I had it conquered, it would pop up in another area of my life: shopping, food, or exercise. They all had a price, but the feeling of being in love was the most expensive, as the Femme Fatale began to emerge again, only this time, in force.

The signs were abundant, from always searching for a romantic relationship to finding it distressing, even frightening, to be alone, from confusing new romances with love to the inability to stay in a relationship when the newness wore off. I was in love with the idea of being in love.

Credit that to dopamine, the neurotransmitter responsible for stimulating the brain by triggering that euphoric and heavenly sensation of walking on cloud nine. The high of the dopamine diminishes after time, and when it does, so do the feelings for romantic interests. Caroline Myss discusses the Femme Fatale in *The Power of Archetypes*; she says actions such as this are just like catnip and describes me: when the high wears off, the woman is on to the next man.

The aspect of my shadow here was so deeply rooted in fear, I was unable to control my behavior. Just like alcohol, I was powerless over relationships. Only when I discovered my own mother's abandonment as a child, learning that her primal need for love, nurturing, and physical safety was ignored, could I then make sense of my inability to form an intimate relationship.

This pattern of behavior was like that of a hamster on a wheel, spinning in circles, expending its energy with nothing to show for it. Each time I met someone new, sparks ignited like fireworks, but sooner rather than later, the fire would smolder and burn out.

If the definition of insanity is doing the same thing over and over again, expecting different results, then I was insane. I would continually pick emotionally unavailable men I was physically attracted to and expect to have an intimate, long-lasting relationship. What was wrong with me?

My uncle has many quotes associated with his name, known as "Father Bill-isms," and besides telling me my picker was broken, he said, "Two sickies don't make a wellie," and "An addict is incapable of having an intimate, loving relationship with themselves, others, the universe, and God." I was in complete and total denial, and had no clue as to how sick I was.

Self-esteem was a foreign concept to me. In psychology, self-esteem is a person's overall sense of self-worth or personal value. The evaluation I had of myself was one of unworthiness, due in part to my hiding under a cover of guilt and shame, as well as being starved for love. My craving for someone to love me had no bounds; it seemed impossible.

I discovered it would never occur until I first learned to love myself. It reminds me of another saying from Father Bill and AA: "Let us love you until you are capable of loving yourself." Subsequently, for the next thirteen years, I kept up a constant battle to acquire this Holy Grail of self-love, only to consistently miss the mark.

~~~~~~~~

In early September 1987, my life began to unravel in every aspect; my first Saturn Return, the astrological phenomenon that occurs between the ages of twenty-eight and thirty, when the planet Saturn returns to the same point in the sky it was in when you were born, cracked its whip. Saturn is known as the taskmaster planet in astrology, the planetary disciplinarian, and like a cosmic life coach, it will teach you to walk through your fears and pain.

You may go through a total career change and have to start all over again or end an important relationship. Saturn Return, which lasts two and a half to three years, also brings pressure to change your attitudes about your parents or those in authority, develop a new relationship with God, or begin a spiritual path.

The first Saturn Return is a time of serious self-examination, where you'll have to face your problems and deal with them actively. You are being asked, "Who are you?" and "Where are you going?" Any masks you've worn will begin to work against you, as you begin to get honest about yourself and answer these simple questions.

And indeed, when I was twenty-nine, everything around me started to crumble, resulting in turmoil. My losses were many and included family members, a professional career, and even a romantic relationship, all within a six-month period.

The starting point for the dismantling of my external world occurred on September 8, when my grandmother passed away. Not even three weeks went by when I received a phone call from my supervisor, who told me the company decided to part ways with me. When I asked why he called versus meeting with me, the answer was disturbing: he thought I would cry, and he didn't want to be a part of a scene.

A few months later, just before Christmas, I ended a year-long relationship with Steve because he was noncommittal, even though he consistently led his life to please me, and I wasn't able to communicate my feelings for him. The final straw that led me to question everything about life took place on February 8 of the following year, when I sat at my brother's bedside and watched him take his last breath.

The weight of holding up my parents for the past four years crushed me, along with the mask of being strong. Yielding to the anguish I carried inside, I began to scream at the top of my lungs. I was bereft of my senses as I entered another black hole, uncontrollably howling until given medication to alleviate the stress.

~~~~~~~~

In April 1988, my eyes began to cross involuntarily, which also occurred right after lightning struck me. Only this time, the spasms returned with a vengeance and occurred much more frequently, up to twenty-five times during the course of a day. They remained active through the summer when I was on a business/pleasure trip in Cancun with my new employer, a Fortune 500 company and leader in industrial lubricants. As I mentioned that experience over dinner with my colleagues, a severe thunderstorm began to develop. Having mentioned to someone earlier in the evening about being struck by lightning, they suggested, "Do you think the lightning strike is causing your spasms?" The question initiated the connection between the seizure-like twitches and the lightning strike to become apparent.

Hmmm. There must be some truth in that, I thought, and I was anxious to return home to see if they were connected. I made an appointment with a well-known and respected neurologist, and after I completed a mountain of forms, he gave me a full physical checkup. He was very curious, of course, because doctors rarely have a patient who's been struck by lightning.

After my initial consultation and general electroencephalogram (EEG), he said he would like me to undergo a twenty-four-hour EEG, a test that measures and records the electrical activity of the brain over the course of a day and night. Electrodes, or specialized sensors, are attached to the head and connected to a computer. The computer, in turn, records this activity on a monitor as wavy lines. Certain conditions, such as seizures, can be detected by the changes in the normal pattern of the brain's electrical activity.

In my situation, I had the sensors attached to my scalp and the wires connected to a small box secured at my waist. Each time I had a spasm where my eyes crossed, I was instructed to push the button on the EEG recorder. As I was all wired up and ready to leave, I asked the doctor if I could wear a sun hat. The answer was a resounding no, as it would interfere with the recording process. With a morose attitude, I walked out of the office to my car, feeling like Martin from *My Favorite Martian*.

For the next twenty-four hours, I pressed the button on the recorder each time I felt a twitch. With nothing better to do, I made a cup of tea and settled in with a fascinating book. I certainly wasn't about to go to dancing or even to the corner store looking like this. I wasn't going anywhere until I returned to the doctor's office to remove the apparatus. My gratitude increased with each sticky electrode that was removed. In fact, I could not wait to go home, shower, and wash away the glue that stuck to my scalp and hair.

After a week, I learned of the ambulatory EEG results. The neurologist analyzed the findings and concluded I had ocular convergence spasms, a rare condition where the eyes intermittently converge or turn toward each other, like looking cross-eyed. There is very little known about this disorder, but it was evident through the EEG that the electrical impulses in my brain were misfiring, causing my eyes to converge.

He was 99 percent certain the cause was from the lightning strike I incurred years earlier and gave me two options: the first was to take Dilantin, a medication mostly prescribed for epilepsy. This choice prevented me from operating a car, so I immediately ruled it out, as my career in outside sales required me to drive.

The other option I had was to do nothing. My neurologist felt that although the spasms may continue to increase over time, there was the same possibility they may eventually fade away entirely. In short, there was no definitive answer. Leaving the office, I felt a bit dejected, uncertain about the future of these spasms.

My despondency lifted, however, as the interval between the incidents occurring increased, resulting in fewer and less-intense seizures. Within six months, there were very few of them. However, as the years passed, severe unexplained nerve pain would arise, side effects that also were a result from the lightning entering my body.

~~~~~~~~

Thinking the worst of life was behind me, two years later, I found myself in a relationship with Billy, who was eight years my junior. Despite our age difference, we spent a lot of time enjoying many of life's treasures. We water-skied on the Delaware River. I met his parents and family, went to his nephew's christening, and attended his cousin's wedding, where I caught the bouquet. But when we went to the St. Anthony's Italian festival, I saw his generous heart of gold and fell in love; he gave the arcade tickets we won to several children so they could redeem them for a prize.

Everything was unfolding in a manner I never experienced before. I can't honestly say what the difference was, but there was one. Perhaps it was Billy's age or his upbringing. Whatever it was, I felt completely at peace and free to be myself, which was a foreign feeling for me. Even when I told him I loved him, and he replied he wasn't ready to say that yet, it didn't cause resentment to build, the way it had in the past.

And then, in the blink of an eye, he was gone.

I knew something was wrong when he didn't call on the Fourth of July. We had plans to take the boat out to Penn's Landing and watch the fireworks. I kept calling his apartment, but there was no answer; not even his roommate was home. The next day, my stomach was heaving from nerves; I knew something terrible had happened.

It was midafternoon when I got the call. My boyfriend's roommate told me that JeffSTAT, the Critical Care Support for Thomas Jefferson University Medical Center, airlifted Billy to the hospital; he had been hit by a drunk driver two nights before. My entire world stopped on a dime; I was hyperventilating and couldn't breathe. Thank goodness, my dad was home and drove me straight up to the hospital, doing his best to comfort me. It was an impossible task, as I was inconsolable; I feared the worst.

When I arrived and saw the look on his parents' faces, I knew it was severe. I didn't know how grave it was until the doctor allowed me to enter his room to visit him. Death, once again, stared me straight on. There was a shunt inserted into his brain, his left arm was in a cast, as was his left leg. Numerous injuries made it difficult to identify him. I sat by his bedside and wept.

He died less than a week later. His parents were very accepting of me, considering the brief time we were together, as well as our age difference; I was thirty-two; he was just twenty-four. Wanting to be with them at both the viewing and funeral, I reserved a hotel room for the weekend. Lost and in pain, I couldn't do anything but grieve. How many losses can someone endure in life?

Together, these milestones embodied everything in my life, except for the spiritual realm. Did the thought of picking up a drink after seven years of abstinence flow through my head? Of course it did, but the one spiritual axiom I held firmly to and believed was this: God stood in front of me, Jesus was by my side, and the Holy Spirit was kicking me in the butt.

Sometimes, the only thing that stands between you and a drink is God.

CHAPTER 9

Love at First Sight

"No one falls in love by choice; it is by chance. No one stays in love by
chance; it is by work. And no one falls out of love by chance;
it is by choice."
~ Unknown ~

It happened on my birthday, a Saturday night, the last day in April 1992. To celebrate the occasion, four friends took me out for a night on the town full of revelry, laughter, and dance. Midway through the festive evening, as my confidantes were savoring their adult beverages, I sipped my soda, thinking how blessed I was to be with people who loved me.

We were whooping it up and cracking jokes at each other's expense, when Karen, one of my friends, told me to look to my right. I turned my head in the direction she pointed; there was a man looking in my direction, and as my gaze met his, our eyes locked. I was mesmerized.

As we stared deeply into each other's eyes, sweat began to form at the nape of my neck; my heart stopped and then pounded furiously in my chest. A surge pulsed through my entire body that left the hairs on my arms upright, as I stood there shaking, revisiting the vivid memory of when I was struck by lightning years before.

I wondered if this is what love at first sight, feels like because it was the most stimulating physical response I ever experienced from a look. Our eyes met with such depth and intensity; it was impossible to look away.

His eyes were dark, almost piercing, but they had a soft, gentle quality to them that welcomed my attention. Dressed in jeans and a denim jacket, sporting a jet-black mustache that was only slightly darker than his hair, he could pass for the Marlboro Man; my Marlboro Man.

A sharp jab to my rib cage momentarily broke the spell I was under; I instantly knew it was Karen's elbow, as she was always the provocateur. Before I could say a word, she spoke with more command than suggestion: "Debbie, you need to hurry over there and meet him. Now."

It was Karen in action; she noticed the expression on my face when our eyes met, lingering in a laser-like focus, and was intent on playing matchmaker. Sighing, I pleaded with her for a few minutes to catch my breath, as the visual encounter had knocked the wind out of me.

Taking a deep breath of air bolstered my courage, and I made my way across the dance floor to the bar, where this handsome man stood.

With butterflies in my stomach, I said "Hello," but his response was unintelligible. Feeling foolish, I began to retrace my steps and retreat.

As I turned away, I heard a voice close to the Marlboro Man shout out with a foreign accent, "Wait, please. Karl does not speak English. He is German. My name is Hans, and I can interpret English for him."

Did I hear right?

This revelation threw me for a loop, leaving my thoughts in disarray. I was speechless. Honestly, how in the world was I going to communicate with … what was his name? Karl? As if he were a mentalist, Hans interrupted my baffled ruminations, saying he would interpret the conversation for us.

It was, to put it mildly, a very intriguing proposal, and for the next hour, Karl and I communicated via Hans. I discovered he was from a small village near Heilbronn and was in the United States on a work visa from Audi; he inspected all the new cars arriving at the Port of Wilmington. During our three-way conversation, every now and then, I would secretly glance over to my friends who, while smiling happily, also made funny faces at me. I got no respect.

When I went to excuse myself to rejoin my party, I heard Karl ask Hans something in German; Hans relayed that Karl wanted to see me again.

Curious, I asked, "When?" and he replied, "Tomorrow night."

Agreeing to meet the next evening in front of a nearby sports bar, I bid them farewell and reunited with my gal pals. My birthday bash was winding down, and the night was ending, but my infatuation and desire were just beginning.

We scheduled our rendezvous at Tailgates for eight o'clock, and when I arrived, Karl was standing outside the entrance, smoking a cigarette. There was a flutter in my belly as I approached him, considering I did not have the faintest idea what our plans were, not to mention how we were to converse.

Karl said, *"Hallo,"* and gestured to me. By some means, I got the picture he wanted me to follow him, so I did. Sitting in the driver's seat of my car, I shook my head, resolving I must have a screw loose to go to an unknown location with a foreign man and one who couldn't speak a lick of English, either.

Intense desire and euphoria flooded my inner being as I drove behind his car. Still unclear about our destination, a sense of foreboding loomed in the air until it registered: Karl had mentioned where their apartments were the night before, and he was headed in that direction now. We weren't going *out* on a date, rather, we were staying in.

Aware of the implied message when someone invites you back to their place, I was neither prepared for it nor ready to take my leave. I was mesmerized as this attractive man placed me in a trancelike state. What was it that pulled me toward him with the force of a magnet?

We had chemistry: the emotion two people get when they share a significant connection and have the urge to be with each other. There was *a je ne sais quoi* to it, and one I couldn't verbalize. I felt only a flickering of my heart that intensified with each passing minute.

Perhaps it was his self-confidence and the way he carried himself that sparked my desire; he was unlike any man I'd ever met. He was very different; not only was he from a different country and spoke a different language, but the way he stared into my eyes seemed vastly different, as well. It felt as if he was peering into the window of my soul.

Karl took my hand and led me up two flights of stairs to his apartment. That mixed bag of feelings was beginning to swirl again and gradually intensified as he closed the door and pulled my body close to his. Looking down at me with a soft gaze, he lifted my chin, so our lips would touch. His kiss, so sensual, left me wanting for more; I was at his mercy.

As Karl guided me through another door, the one leading to his bedroom, I lost all sense of decorum. *Oh, my God*, I thought, as he laid me down on the bed, *this is surreal. We haven't even spoken a word to each other.* It wasn't necessary; we had our own language, the language of love.

Eventually, after several hours (it seemed to go on forever), I found myself back in my car, driving home. Was this all a dream? Shaking my head, fully awake and aware of what just happened, I berated myself for the indiscretion. Although I was disenchanted with the lack of self-control, my feelings could not be denied: giddiness, titillation, and infatuation occurred simultaneously, causing my mind to race, rendering me sleepless.

The lack of sleep was trivial in comparison with the uncertainty of seeing him again.

The following day fared no better, as my concentration was also deficient. Memories from the previous evening streamed into my consciousness, invading my thoughts. Doing my best to let them go, they only circled back again. The tennis match of daydreams volleying back and forth in my head left me torn. Would I see him again? Yes, I thought, because he must feel the same about me. No, it was just a one-night stand for him.

This conflict continued throughout the day and left me in a state of agony until I received a call from Hans; Karl was interested in seeing me again. The game in my head was over, and I won. Thoughts of infatuation swelled as the thought of a new love story emerged. The whirlwind pace also brought with it the fear that the other shoe would drop.

Obviously, there were challenges to overcome; there were the language barrier and cultural differences, as well as the fact he was here on a work visa that expired the end of June. I minimized these complications, as my focus was on ensuring the success of the relationship, and that required me to take swift action. I needed to learn German.

I accepted Karl's invitation. Hans asked me several more questions, to which I answered yes: we can visit New York City, I would drive, and finally, yes, I would purchase an English-German dictionary. Hans looked forward to taking a bite out of the Big Apple, as well, and it made sense for him to come along, since Karl and I still found it out of the question to have a meaningful conversation. Scheduling the adventure for the upcoming weekend, I imagined us exploring the city; I hoped it would be an enjoyable time.

On my way to pick up my two fellow travelers, I stopped and bought two easy-to-learn German books, each varying slightly from the other. Reservations mildly tempered my enthusiasm to revisit New York City. Would the three of us be compatible? Would we agree or argue about what to see, do, and eat? Although seeming to be minor, they could be make-or-break decisions, affecting the atmosphere surrounding us, particularly when spending ten hours with near-strangers.

The sunshine was abundant and furnished us with ample warmth to enjoy the first Saturday in May; it was a picture-perfect day. After parking in an underground garage, we happily set out on foot. First on the agenda to visit was the Statue of Liberty. Walking to the destination, I recited my first German words to Karl: *"Ich murtoch ein eiss."* The translation was, "I would like an ice cream." He appreciated the gesture and the initiative I took to learn it. My Student archetype was thriving.

After the ice cream break, Karl reached for my hand, giving it a slight squeeze as we strolled up Fifth Avenue. My captivation for this man deepened by the minute. Or was it a primal sexual urge, the attraction that feels chemical, like a drug? The Addict was shrewd, shadowing the purely physical desire with illusion of a deeper connection.

Self-deception was rampant; I honestly believed I felt a different energy the first time our eyes locked, like bullhorns in a fight. It was a sense of knowing. A sense of knowing? If I had any sense of knowing, I would have downplayed my emotional state and realized I have what the Urban Dictionary calls SBS: Shiny

Ball Syndrome. The Addict taunted me, letting me know I would stumble and fall again.

Shifting back to the present, I pinched myself as I glanced around. It wasn't a dream; I was with a man who instantly captured my heart, and we were about to visit Ellis Island and the Statue of Liberty. The storybook romance I always dreamed of was blossoming before my eyes, only I saw something that wasn't there. My imagination continued to grow, seeing Karl for more than what he was. It wasn't his fault; it was my longing to have the whole love story that clouded my vision.

As the day wore on, our familiarity with each other showed through increased physical intimacy: constantly holding hands, arms draped around each other's shoulders, even a piggyback ride with the Twin Towers in the background. Smiles and twinkles in our eyes made it obvious to anyone around we were a couple in love.

~~~~~~~~

The following two months of our romance had many ups and downs, and more unexpected twists and turns than a roller-coaster ride. After the New York City tour, I moved into Karl's apartment. Things were great, at first. We spent time getting to know each other and enjoyed the newness of the relationship.

To look past a person's good behavior and see them for who they truly are is itself a challenge. Include a language barrier, and you have a recipe for chaos. Add a dash of alcohol on one side to the mix, and huge arguments erupt. The emotional ride always left me in tears, as the thought that this fairy tale would crash and burn crushed me.

Several times, I called my father, who on one occasion came to the apartment and had a sit-down conversation with Karl and then with me. Whatever my dad said positively influenced him, as it did me; we were both thoughtful and loving for the remainder of his time in the United States.

We were an affable couple, even though we struggled to understand each other. We frequented the Delaware Sangerbund, a social club for people with German ancestry, where we would gather with his coworkers. At other times, we interacted with my friends. It felt like we were climbing to the top of an incredible mountain together. Little did I know an avalanche was going to occur.

In early June, my mother surprised my dad with a sixtieth birthday party. My father loved being the center of attention, almost as much as receiving presents. Karl was my guest at the celebration, and I noticed my parents were forming an attachment to him. I sensed them showing fondness toward Karl; it appeared to help them through their grieving process from the loss of my brother, Donnie.

However, there was a problem: Karl couldn't remain in the United States. The information not only felt like a sucker punch to my solar plexus, it also initiated a surge of fear that pulsated throughout my body. It also left me confused. On the one hand, Karl was telling me he loved me; I was his American Dream girl, and on the other, he lived in Germany, and his visa was expiring.

What was I supposed to do now that I'd fallen in love with him, just let him go? No, I was going to go the distance, wherever that led. However, the Addict wanted more control than ever, and I felt engulfed by a wave of despair, which eventually landed me in a psychiatric hospital.

The fear within me reared its ugly head whenever the thought of Karl's departure date came to mind: fear of abandonment, fear of losing the love of my life, fear of another heartbreak, fear of not being good enough. With only a week or so left before he returned to Germany, I became frantic with worry, convinced beyond a doubt I would never see him again.

Not wanting to feel the pain and loss, two days before he was to leave, I swallowed twenty-one of my dad's Valium. Shortly after ingesting the pills, I told Karen what I had done, and she demanded I tell my mother, who called 911.

My Addict archetype fell deeper in the shadow. This entity caused obsessive passion within my psyche. This suicide attempt was a destructive force, both physically and mentally. How was I to overcome this shadow? It would take another eight years of banging my head against a brick wall until I raised my awareness and came into the light.

The emergency responders directed Karen to take me to the ER for treatment. Once there, to induce vomiting and remove any of the remaining sedatives in my stomach, I needed to drink a charcoal-like substance. The experience was one of the most unpleasant ones in my life and further strengthened my self-destructive behavior by not recognizing the Saboteur at work.

The deeper consequence of my decision became apparent when the nurse told me I would be involuntarily committed to Rockwood, a psychiatric treatment center, for a seventy-two-hour observation. Knowing I hadn't intended to commit suicide, I became angry and defiant at the order.

"No way. I'm not going," I firmly avowed, hoping to expunge my foolish mistake. Unable to do so, I was forced to concede; the EMTs transported me to the institution. Hopelessness set in; not only was I being held against my will, but Karl would leave before I was released. The thought of not seeing him again sunk me deeper into a depression that encompassed both my physical body and inner soul. I shut down, crawling inward to the safety of my imaginary world. It was impossible for me to stay in touch with everyday life now; a piece of me died, and I needed to withdrawal.

Alone in a room with no view, my thoughts led me to review my past. *Here I go again,* I mused, *on the roller coaster of love. The highs are thrilling; the lows are heartbreaking. My life has a way of emulating that amusement park ride. Not only am I addicted to alcohol, but I'm addicted to love as well, specifically, addicted to falling in love.* The act of falling in love makes sense to me now, but it didn't then.

Isolation was a coping mechanism for me when confined; I ventured out of my room only when mandated to see the therapist or obtain medical attention. The first night in seclusion was a restless one for me.

The next day, however, I had visitors. My parents brought along a surprise: Karl! When I saw him standing in the doorway, my heart skipped a beat. We hugged, holding on like there was no tomorrow. It wasn't until we professed our love for each other that we began to loosen our grip and realize the extent of our situation.

Karl was leaving the following day, flying back home to Germany, while at the same time, I was detained in a mental facility. We faced many uncertain questions that left our future up in the air. The worst part was not knowing what was in store for us.

After the visit with my parents and Karl, I crawled into bed and cried like never before. If felt like my heart was ripped out of my chest. The Victim archetype, feeling wronged, shouted, "God, why are you doing this to me? I'm a decent person." I even tried to bargain with Him.

He must have heard my plea because just when I was coming to terms with my plight, an orderly entered the room and told me my insurance did not cover the hospital expense. They were going to transfer me to another location. *Oh, no they weren't,*

I thought. *I'm going home.* I called my parents to come pick me up and take me home, signing myself out against medical advice (AMA).

I would see Karl off, after all.

The following day was bittersweet. Sweet, because I saw Karl and told him I loved him before he left; bitter because not only was he leaving the country, he was also leaving me in the dark. Knowing my hands were tied sent me deeper into depression.

We faced an implausible scenario: how could we continue our relationship? What were the chances of it surviving a few visits here and there? Slim to none, in my mind. The more I thought about the impossibility, the more despondent I became.

July dragged on and on and on. Each day weighed heavier than the previous one. After a couple weeks, my friend Karen, the one who pushed me into the initial meeting with Karl, suggested we go on a road trip to Virginia Beach. Wanting to wallow in my sorrow and self-pity, I was resolute about not going.

Karen, the great persuader, told me I needed to get on with my life and not wait around for what might be. She was right; two weeks had passed since Karl left, and I hadn't had a phone call or letter from him. I agreed to go; after packing a bag, we hit the road.

The trip to the beach did help pass the time, although mentally, I was still in a state of anxiety, which resulted from not having a clear picture of future decisions that needed to be made. Angst: I loathed the feeling, despite the fact I should be used to it. I was in love, again. And once more, I fell into my repetitive pattern of thinking: *This time, it was different; he was different.* The same thoughts, however, continued to plague me: *Would I live happily ever after, or would my world come crashing down, again?*

~~~~~~~~

One day in early August, my phone rang. It was Karl. My heart jumped straight to my throat, and I could feel my breath tighten, like a boa constrictor squeezing its prey. It relaxed and floated back into place when he conveyed his news: he loved me and wanted to marry me. *Marry me? Was I dreaming?*

Never before in my life had a man even hinted at the prospect of marriage. My heart sang while my insides danced. The revelation would change my life, or so I thought. Changing your external environment doesn't guarantee that your internal world will follow suit. Who cares? All I knew was, Karl loved me enough to marry me.

From that day forward, we wrote each other letters, sent lovey-dovey cards and faxes, and spoke on the phone. Communicating was still confusing, as neither of us knew the other's language enough to speak or write it fluently. It didn't matter; we had our own language of love to sustain us through our time apart.

The Addict's power still exerted its control over me; I was in love with the idea of being in love. My heart was telling me yes, this was what I've always fantasized about, while my head said no, our chances for marriage were slim to none. This incongruence caused me to choose unwisely. The Femme Fatale's provocation caused further disarray, leading me to think I needed to have this man. Just as hunters stalk their prey, devouring it when captured, I was on the prowl.

~~~~~~~~

There were numerous details and loose ends to tie up before Karl returned; he estimated it could take a year. For my part, I was to pay off my bills and start saving money for a new home. Time seemed to stand still just when I wished it would fly, and in October, he invited me to visit him in Germany.

After looking over my schedule, I decided to travel the day after Christmas and stay twenty days. I was going to Germany. I had never been to Europe before, let alone experience it with my knight in shining armor. I was living a romantic fairy tale where reality didn't seem to exist. Oh, but it did exist, and I would find out soon enough.

The trip was fast approaching. My castles in the air were, in fact, materializing, and with them was a lingering optimism of where life was taking me. My mind overflowed with thoughts, as I created various scenarios of our adventures. It was, in fact, racing like it usually did, but now it was in the Indy 500.

Highlighting and tabbing pages in my travel guide was the Student in me, but the desire to see and do everything allowed the Addict to thrive, as well. Doing my best to calm my mind, I took a deep breath and looked away from the book. It was only a temporary respite. Twenty years would pass before my heightened mental activity would be diagnosed; not only did I have ADHD, I had ADHD with impulsivity. Adding this element to the Addict, it was clear to see the reason for its strength.

My thoughts focused back on Karl. How would I feel when I saw him again, after six months apart? Would I still have the same feelings? Would my love be the same? Would I love him more, or less? In my mind, I loved him, but these questions cast a shadow of doubt that lingered over my head. Based on my past experiences, I wasn't 100 percent certain of anything.

One thing I knew for sure: I wanted to be certain. I wanted to change the behavior of my past, so my future would be free of chaos. The only problem was, I still didn't know how to change. I consistently tried to find the key to unlock it without success.

The date of my departure arrived. The whole gamut of emotions created a disturbance inside of me: anxiety, excitement, fear, love, and happiness. Despite the lengthy flight, sleep escaped me. My nerves were frazzled, and upon landing, my stomach churned. Fear topped off these emotions and kept me shackled like a prisoner, despite struggling to relax. I disembarked the plane and headed to the terminal.

My heart, beating a mile a minute, suddenly stopped when I spotted Karl waiting for me. His eyes overflowed with love, and he held a single red rose. Fear melted away when we approached each other, and just like a storybook romance, he wrapped his arms around me and gave me his warmest hug. He then lowered his face to mine and kissed me. I became lost in the moment; nothing else existed.

We reluctantly released our hold and gazed into each other's eyes. When the deep love he held in them penetrated mine, I melted.

"I love you, my American Dream girl," he whispered.

"I love you too," I replied softly.

He gently took my hand, placing his on top, and we headed through Frankfurt's airport to baggage claim. The churning sensation in my stomach began to ease when I let go of my stress. It was true; I was here in Germany with Karl.

~~~~~~~~

The following April, during my second trip to Germany, I experienced an emotional breakdown. With the security of marriage in the offing, the wounds from my past traumas were triggered, bringing them to the surface and interfering with my ability to be intimate with Karl. My negative reactions to his kisses were intense and out of proportion; flashbacks replayed the horrors of my past. No matter how I struggled to erase them from my mind, they proved too powerful.

After numerous failed attempts, I told Karl to take me to the airport; I thought I should call off the engagement. He reluctantly drove me to the Frankfurt Sheraton, located in the airport, but was adamant that I call my parents, who were unaware of the triggering assaults, and let them know what was happening before I left.

That decision changed everything. My mother and dad comforted me and suggested I receive counseling for the abuse upon my return home. The weight of holding onto the pain was suddenly released, allowing me to relax and enjoy the remainder of my visit with Karl. For now, everything was back to normal. When I arrived back home, I immediately scheduled an appointment with a therapist specializing in sexual abuse and enrolled in a six-week program based on Ellen Bass and Laura Davis's book, *The Courage to Heal*.

The program consisted of a small group of women, who had all experienced some type of childhood sexual trauma. We broke into groups and participated in the various techniques from the book, such as guided imagery and body-centered practices. I continued to do the work at home every night for the duration of the series, and when it was over, I felt hope that I would heal from these wounds.

~~~~~~~~

Karl arrived in the United States on July 3, 1993. In petitioning for a fiancé visa, one of the stipulations the United States Citizens and Immigration Services (USCIS) required was to show we planned to marry within ninety days. Since our wedding was set for October 30, and not subject to change, his debarkation was clearly out of the required time frame we had to marry. To prevent Karl from deportation, we married in a civil ceremony officiated by the mayor of Wilmington. My parents and best friend joined us.

There was an Action News van out front with a bevy of commotion. We didn't know it at the time, but the mayor was meeting with a well-known professional basketball player from

Philadelphia about a waterfront project. The pro athlete saw we were getting married and offered to stay for a photograph. What a fortunate stroke of serendipity.

~~~~~~~~

After our designated wedding and honeymoon, Karl and I settled into our new apartment. Life had the usual happenings, happy times, as well as challenging ones, but we were content. It wasn't easy, however, with the language and culture barriers, and I lost my patience more than a few times.

By the end of our first year of marriage, we had paid off my debt and saved enough money to purchase a new home. Karl and I looked at existing homes but decided on new construction. Life was good, until shortly after we moved in.

Before long, my breakthrough would cause our breakup.

CHAPTER 10

Breakthrough

Sometimes it takes an overwhelming breakdown
to have an undeniable breakthrough.
~ Unknown ~

We moved into a beautiful three-bedroom colonial situated on one of the largest lots in the development of Rutledge, just outside of New Castle, Delaware. It was August 1994 and a happy time, a time where everything was new, and we would write our story. I was eager to become a housewife and live the suburban life. Only that didn't happen.

A month after moving in, I was invited to a neighbor's candle party. I saw the opportunity to earn extra income, so I signed up to be a representative. Wanting the ability to purchase a few extras for the house, I thought Karl would be grateful, but I was wrong. We began to argue, and there were times I didn't want to be married anymore. It felt like all the love was being drained out of me.

Within a few months, just after Christmas, Karl began to sleep in the guest bedroom. It was hard to imagine; we had broken down as a couple and drifted apart so quickly. I tried my best to be a loving wife, as did Karl a loving husband, but we just could not compromise on key issues, such as finances, sex, and time spent together. I felt broken, fragmented, and not fully healed from the traumatic wounds of my past.

My uncle, Father Bill Hultberg, the spiritual advisor at the Caron Foundation, a drug and alcohol rehabilitation center, suggested I enter Breakthrough, their five-day treatment program to address my codependency issues and deal with my traumatic past. I was granted a scholarship for the intensive curriculum, which equaled two years of therapy, and he felt it was essential to take part in this healing workshop to become whole again. I agreed, and so in April 1995, I entered Breakthrough, the life-coaching program. Karl also thought that I should go, especially if it helped our relationship.

After I arrived at Caron and checked in, an aide escorted me to my room. There were no distractions such as televisions or phones to divert our attention from the work we were about to tackle. Paula, my roommate, was a small redhead with a kindhearted nature. There were eighteen other patients in our group.

None of us had any sense of the dynamic transformations that were about to occur: the raw emotions that would be exposed, leaving us bare; the tears that would flow; the healing that would take place. The approach Caron used was extremely safe and confidential. The men and women assembled separately, with broken hearts and bankrupt spirits, but left united, with mended hearts and souls embracing deep self-love.

For the intensely integrated recovery and psychodrama sections of the program, the twenty patients were separated into two groups: A and B. One exercise involved psychodrama, where each of us assigned someone in the group to be the person we were angry with. We then had to speak to that individual, revealing the wounds they had caused or trauma they had inflicted. Whenever we felt compelled to express or release our pent-up anger and rage, we pummeled a large pillow using padded sticks.

As I sat watching the drama unfold, I remember thinking, *you're not going to get me up in front of everybody to act out like that. No way is that going to happen.* I was frozen, petrified, my feelings deadened. I didn't want to feel the emotional pain I had stuffed deep inside and concealed for the past twenty years. *No. No. No. I am not going to participate.*

As the counselor turned and faced me, her eyes held such compassion and grace, any fear of distress melted away. In my heart, I knew if I had any expectation of healing, I needed to walk through my fear and play the part. Desperate to achieve this outcome, I began to choose people to act like my mother, my father, and my sexual offenders.

As the process began, I noticed myself slide into character, asking the questions I had yearned to hear answers for all these years. As if there were no one else in the room, I was oblivious to anyone or anything, save my inner turmoil.

"Where were you, Mommy and Daddy? Where were you when I needed your protection? Why weren't you there for me?" The boiling rage inside of me began to unlock; I felt it rise from my solar plexus up through my chest, reaching my throat, and out my mouth, as I screamed, "Why, why, why didn't you protect me?"

Slamming the stick into the pillow with such force, even I was stunned at the amount of power I yielded. As I continued to beat the pillow, I yelled, "Fuck you. Fuck you. Fuck you!"

Tears streamed down my cheeks, and I tasted their saltiness as they slid into my mouth. My head fell to my knees as I crumpled over like a rag doll and began to sob uncontrollably. How did I do that? I felt an intense desire to understand the gripping force behind my action. It was as if a higher power had entered my soul, infusing me with the courage to stand up to and confront my pain, my shame, my blemishes, head-on. The role-play therapy not only left me drained, stunned, and bewildered; it also depleted all my remaining energy.

Gingerly, I crawled back to my place on the floor, quietly observing the next person as she took her turn. Each time the process was repeated, I was utterly overwhelmed as each one opened up wounds so raw, they would unnerve an ordinary person. Emotions laden with disgrace and remorse were directly challenged, diminished, and replaced by forgiveness and acceptance, along with hope and love. Transformations were transpiring in this moment; miracles took place before our very eyes, as healing at its highest level presented itself.

The work left me exhausted, yet I could feel myself begin to let go of the psychic weight that had anchored me for years. Under the tutelage of Caroline Myss, I would learn that weight equals wait; the heavier your psychic weight, the longer the wait to manifest or heal. Freedom was just around the corner, and I was intent on obtaining it.

When everyone had finished role-playing for the psychodrama exercise, the group united, giving hugs and words of praise to help us increase our self-love and self-esteem. I trusted the process, not only because the therapist told me to, but because I felt safe in doing so.

I felt safe. The feeling was foreign to me, and the situation was baffling. Here, in the midst of strangers, men and women who all suffered from some form of addiction, I felt safe. Because we had bared our souls, exposing our most intimate experiences and secrets without being judged, we bonded to each other with a trust far exceeding any I had ever known. Most of the time we shared was spent scaling the magnificent mountain of recovery and the spiritual path to healing. Little did we know that we were in for the journey of our lives.

Regression therapy was also part of the treatment plan. For this method, we were instructed to sit or lie down in a comfortable position, as music played softly in the background, then a soft voice guided us back to our childhoods.

When I focused on my six-year-old self, there was a protective bubble around her. As I held her tiny hand in mine, we silently walked down a long, winding path through the woods. There were endless vibrant flowers, unfamiliar plants, an assortment of resplendent butterflies and birds, as the sunlight shimmered through tall, shady trees. We ambled alongside a stream. The sound of water flowing over the rocks was relaxing.

A footbridge soon appeared, and after we crossed a babbling brook, we came to a roving meadow filled with wildflowers, brilliant in every color of the rainbow. While the energy from that vibrancy pierced straight through the bubble, it also safeguarded me from any harm. My little girl and I frolicked through the blossoms, resting briefly every now and again, to be fully present and drink in God's miraculous creations. The horizon drew my attention; I could see the house where I grew up. Continuing to grasp my child's hand, I gave an encouraging squeeze every so often, to assure her it was safe. I was her protector, her guardian, her advocate.

As we approached the front door of my childhood home, we felt hesitant but still willing to enter. What I remember, and what I noticed in this exercise, was an immaculate house with a place for everything, and everything in its place. A mental picture featured my mother sashaying from one room to another, swiping a white glove across the top of the door frames and baseboards with her forefinger, which she then examined for dust. Terrified that I would dirty something, I ran into my bedroom and crawled into bed, pulling the covers over my head. No one could see me now; I was invisible.

After several more minutes, we were led back to the present, and I felt the wetness of tears on my warm, flushed cheeks. My body trembled as I reconnected with these early childhood memories. This flashback was just the dawning of a memory that was trying to claw its way to the surface. Although that particular memory would not reveal itself for another fifteen years, the healing from past trauma was an enormous breakthrough, in and of itself.

As I was getting ready to go home, my roommate Paula gave me a gift: a bag containing little worry dolls. She explained that whenever I had a problem or issue, I should take one of the dolls out and turn my worry over to it.

After I had finished packing, I reflected on my experiences and the people I had met here, who all left me a better person than when I first arrived. The intimacy and safety I encountered with these individuals far exceeded any I'd had before this moment, including with my family.

My mind wandered to thoughts of home, to the unknown conditions ahead of me. But before they fully formed, a pink cloud (the term used to describe someone in recovery who is too high on life) surrounded me. Since my monumental breakthrough at Caron, I *was* high on life, eager to reenter mainstream living with an entirely new way of thinking and coping skills.

Unsure that our marriage could survive, when I returned home, I reminded myself to live in the present moment. It wasn't that I didn't love Karl. I did, with all my heart. But I was convinced I could not tolerate not only our cultural diversities but other contrary beliefs, which were not beneficial for my personal development. It had come to a point where I needed more encouragement to change and grow.

A patient in my group I became connected with, Sue, offered to drive me home. During the car ride, we exchanged views regarding our Breakthrough insights. We talked about the day twenty strangers met, whose paths otherwise might never have crossed, and the changes that made them close allies, establishing a steadfast bond, impossible to break. Both of us agreed it seemed like a miracle; new life was breathed into us, transforming our spirits.

Our pleasant conversation soon began to ebb, and the closer we came to my front step, the more anxious I became. Despite my pink cloud, fear of the unknown raced through my body. How would I feel, returning to a marriage that I knew was ending? What decisions would I make, and would they be the right ones? These and numerous other questions intruded my thoughts until I recalled a suggestion from therapy: "Don't make any major decisions for at least one year." In just a few short months, I would disregard this post-treatment advice, stumbling down a beaten path covered with more thorns than roses, which pricked me with significant pain during the next several years.

Sue asked whether I would be all right. I nodded but knew otherwise, since I was full of apprehension, coming home to my old life where all I did was exist. It was more a household than a real home, a place where two people resided yet moved in opposite directions.

It was the end of April, and spring was unmistakable, the tulips, hyacinths, and forsythia in full bloom. Their sweet aroma wafted through the air, mingling with the scent of freshly cut grass. Karl was mowing the front lawn. Despite the lingering sweetness in the air, my stomach churned, and a lump formed in my throat. *How on earth am I going to live like this?* I wondered.

My train of thought was interrupted as a smiling Karl waved and shut down the mower. He was delighted to see me and attempted to help with my suitcase. I politely declined, feeling guilty. I didn't want to project any false hope and lead him to believe our marriage was salvageable.

As I stood at the bottom of the stairs, sadness passed through me. Although I had grieved this loss the past week at Caron, it had remained tucked away. Gazing into Karl's eyes now, I admitted I needed to be alone. His smile turned to a frown as he slumped his shoulders and lowered his head.

Climbing the steps, I hauled my luggage upstairs and then proceeded to unpack. It wasn't just dirty clothes I was unpacking; it was also memories of my marriage. Tears welled, and I began to sob. The final curtain was about to fall for us, and I had to let go.

~~~~~~~~

A week passed. As I looked back over the past six months, I realized that when Karl had zigged, I had zagged. From the time he moved out of the master bedroom, our relationship resembled two roommates, not a newly married couple. The arrangement gave the impression of normalcy to outsiders, but I questioned how all of this had happened. We had been married less than a year, pinching pennies and tightening our belts, before purchasing our beautiful home, and now our life together was collapsing in front of us.

In retrospect, I was always pointing a finger at others. I had not focused on my shortcomings. I wasn't to blame; I was the one who'd sought and obtained therapy for healing my traumatic wounds with a counselor and at Caron. I was the one who started going to meetings for Adult Children of Alcoholics (ACOA) after the Breakthrough program.

Even though my parents weren't alcoholics, their parents were, and they both grew up in dysfunctional families where their emotional growth was affected. Neither of them knew how to express their emotions, especially when grieving losses. Not only did I inherit both sets of grandparents' alcoholism, but I also was raised in a home where unhealthy behavior (we were not allowed to have feelings) was the norm.

~~~~~~~~

Five more chaotic and turbulent years would pass before I acquired the wisdom to focus only on myself, rather than trying to fix someone else. The definition of insanity popped up again each time I chose an individual who I perceived as needing to be fixed.

Digging into my past, I recognized a familiar pattern with the men I selected: I either made more money, was more educated, or was older than them. After another ten years on the path of Wounded Healer, I finally understood my father's advice to "never depend on a man." (He hadn't wanted me to end up like my mother, dependent on him for most everything.) Following his advice, I never looked for or chose a loving, nurturing man I could rely on, but the truth was, I desired someone just like him.

CHAPTER 11

On the Rebound

"You're not thinking clearly. By all means, go out with friends, take classes, try new things, begin to build a new life. But don't find another relationship while on the rebound and grieving. It usually creates disaster."

~ Tina B. Tessina ~

Fresh out of Breakthrough, the program that gave me the tools for living a healthy, balanced life, I found myself emotionally raw, although I continued to float on a pink cloud. One Saturday, a couple of weeks after returning home, I went to Porky's, a nightclub in Wilmington. Halfway through the evening, I happened to meet a fellow named Tom, who was leaning against the bar, nursing a Corona.

We chatted a bit, the usual small talk, and what seemed like a few moments in time grew into hours. After describing several experiences of clarity and the shift in perspective I gained, I pointed my finger at Tom's chest and exclaimed, "You want what I have." My emphasis wasn't on him wanting the physical part of me, but on my emotional and spiritual transformation.

We exchanged phone numbers, and shortly after that, I left the club. Driving home, I was lost in my thoughts, creating fantasies, and thinking, *Gee, he's a nice guy*, and then somberly remembered I was still married to Karl.

Karl ... Karl came to America for me, his American Dream girl. There was no denying it; sadly, my feelings had changed. The incident that abruptly turned the light switch off took place in late March, a few weeks before I left for Caron. Of all things, it was pork chops, a meal I spent ninety minutes preparing, that caused my about-face. When he told me they tasted like *scheisse*, I began to cry. I loved Karl, but I wasn't in love with him anymore.

What led to this course of events? We both let life happen instead of addressing issues and differences as they arose. It was a proclivity of mine that would endure for several more years: only initiating changes when there was nowhere to go but up.

The next afternoon was Sunday, and while out running errands, I dialed the number Tom gave me. Hearing a female's voice on the other end of the phone, I drew a breath in but then realized it was his mother. Still upbeat and giddy from the previous night, a sudden surge of emotion swept over me when he said hello. The reason I was calling, I told him, was to see if he was available for lunch the next day. He said he was, so we made plans to meet at TGI Friday's on Concord Pike at noon.

As we continued with our previous conversation, it was necessary for me to let him know I was still married to Karl, explaining we had been living in separate bedrooms for the past five months. Because of this situation, I was unable to enter a romantic relationship with him. However, we could be friends, and I wanted that.

Both the Saboteur and the Prostitute were rearing their ugly heads. These are two Survival archetypes that present us with challenges throughout our lives so we can develop self-esteem. Whenever these opportunities were offered to me, and there were many, their shadows always triumphed.

The Saboteur, Caroline Myss writes, is the "guardian of choice." She goes on to say the core issue for this archetype is fear of inviting change into your life, change that requires you to respond positively. The choices I was making were far from positive; I was running from one relationship to the next, living in the shadow of the Saboteur, and creating self-destructive behavior.

Unaware of the negative impact of my decisions, my emotional affair with Tom began.

We were just friends, I rationalized; it was a nonphysical, platonic relationship. It was essential for me to be convinced of this since I was married, although in name only and on the brink of divorce.

The Prostitute's shadow was so astute, it gradually emerged in my psyche, leading me to believe I could be friends with Tom while still a married woman (happily or not). Even though we spoke frequently, it was the meeting in person that tripped my trigger, soaring my heart rate.

The Prostitute comes into play when our physical safety and survival is threatened. Knowing that my marriage was unable to be salvaged, the fear of financial insecurity loomed overhead. What makes the Prostitute so dangerous is its subtlety, engaging in normal settings where the core issue is how much you are willing to sell of yourself. In my case, it was all of me.

Tom and I would meet at Westminster, a recovery house, specifically in the back room designated for open ACOA meetings, which the general public can attend. I shared often, Tom never shared, but he latched onto everything I said. At one meeting, I revealed my attraction to Mark, a fellow participant of the intimate group from my experience at Caron. I said I wasn't responsible for my thoughts, but I *was* responsible for my actions. Today, I am keenly aware of the obligation to both.

During one meeting, I disclosed that Mark stopped to visit me on his way to Kent County, an hour's drive farther south. An auto dealership hired him to present a motivational seminar to their stagnant sales force. We met at Battery Park in historic New Castle, where we relaxed, picnic style, on a blanket.

We recounted our experiences from Caron, our daily lives since, and the mutual attraction we held, and even flirted with the idea of going to the Sheraton to spend the night together. To be sure, it was enticing, but Mark, also married, agreed it was not an option; we both were firm in the commitment to our vows.

Tom was present at the meeting when I revealed this story, and the aftermath from my confession would come back to haunt me years later. The repercussions were cutting, and I paid a high price for them. However, in my entire life, I never physically betrayed any of my partners.

Now, I am cognizant of the emotional affairs I had in the past with men. My sound judgment was shrouded as I exposed my soul, expressing the frustration my marriage was causing. I needed, if not craved, validation that I was not to blame. The intimacy I felt these two relationships embodied was the missing link in my current union with Karl, for I yearned to be known.

Day after day, week after week, Tom and I continued to see each other at the hour-long meeting at Westminster. Throughout these intervals, we strolled through various public parks, enjoying a scoop of ice cream or just giving our feet a rest and chatting. Holding hands was as far as the physicality went. As I spoke of my life situations, this man listened without passing judgment, forming a bond that rivaled best friends. All I ever wanted was to love and be loved, and I felt this happening.

One Wednesday evening, while at White Clay Creek State Park, we relaxed and listened to a local band play, while enjoying the mixture of various sounds all around: the music from the instruments melding with those of the wildlife within the park. We relished this moment. At the onset of intermission, we decided to take a short walk, and while savoring the stillness in the air, we both became lost in our thoughts.

Although Tom had little doubt I was not happily married and likely would file for divorce, he never made an advance or inappropriate comment to me, alleviating any pressure, which allowed me to lower my guard. The intimacy we shared was a leading factor when considering him a best friend, especially since I didn't have a female best friend. My lack of self-esteem and fear of women evolved from not having the inherent self-worth to create alliances with them.

~~~~~~~~

And then, one evening, it happened. On June 25, a Sunday, Tom suggested we go to TCBY in Fox Run to get a frozen yogurt. After purchasing the ice cream, we returned to his Jeep and indulged in the frosty treats. As I finished the last spoonful of my Snicker Shiver, Tom turned to me and said, with a solemn voice, "Debbie, I can't see you anymore."

Anxiety set in; I could feel my breath being taken away. Time stood still. My mind was unable to comprehend what he just said, leaving me confused and in disbelief. Shaking my head, I thought, *Did I hear right*? With a significant amount of trepidation, I asked, "What do you mean, you can't see me anymore?"

"I can't see you anymore," he replied, "because I've fallen in love with you."

Oh no, I thought. *What am I going to do now? I don't want to lose my best friend.*

My mind began to spin, like a whirling dervish, trying to identify my options. There were only two: stay married to Karl and walk away from the relationship I built with Tom, or change the dynamics of our relationship from one of friendship to a romantic one. I didn't dwell on it long; in less than a minute, I chose the latter. In that instant, life as I knew it was changed forever.

The Prostitute was shrieking with laughter. I had fallen deeper into the shadow and would sell my integrity for financial stability.

Passion ignited, and my heart began to smolder as we finally kissed for the first time. Though I was sitting, my knees were weak when the rush of desire, quelled for so long, came pouring out. I was ecstatic yet petrified. The polarities of these two emotions weighed heavily on me, knowing the choice I just made affected not only my life but also the lives of Karl and Tom. There and then, I knew what I needed to do; I would file for divorce.

For the next few days, I kept this decision to myself, focusing on how I would break the news to Karl with the least amount of drama and heartache. Feeling the dread slowly build, I knew it would be awkward. How could I do this to him? I was, after all, his American Dream girl, the one he left his job and his homeland for.

The culpability and guilt surged over me, pulling on my heartstrings, like the ocean washes over the sand, towing shells on the shoreline back with its powerful ebb. Wanting to avoid feeling contrite about the pain I was about to inflict, I replaced those thoughts with intoxicating ones of Tom, confident I was in love with him.

Finally, the time had come to speak to Karl regarding my decision to end the marriage. He responded as I anticipated, pleading with me to not give up, while proclaiming his love for me. His anxiety was heightened by a major concern: that he would be deported back to Germany if we were to divorce before the required two-year mark.

Under these circumstances, I agreed to postpone filing until our two-year anniversary at the end of July. My emotions stretched through me, ready to snap. At one extent, there was profound sadness, as the most meaningful relationship I've ever had was ending, and I found myself in a state of bereavement. On the other side, there was an exquisite sense of joy that arose from the onset of a new partnership, with all the hopes and dreams of a beautiful life together.

My Survival archetypes played an integral role here, especially the Saboteur. "Like the Victim and the Prostitute, the Saboteur is made up of the fears and issues related to low self-esteem that cause you to make choices in life that block your own empowerment," Myss writes. She adds, "When you face this archetype, as with all the others, you learn to heed these warnings, saving yourself untold grief from making the same mistakes over and over. Ignore it, and the shadow Saboteur will manifest in the form of self-destructive behavior."

Myss's words describe my behavior to a tee; I still had low self-esteem and made choices that kept me from becoming empowered. Choosing to rebound from one relationship to the next prevented me, at the very least, from the necessary time to heal.

The pattern in my life consisted of choosing the same type of man (emotionally unavailable, codependent, or in need of fixing) and expecting different results, namely a healthy relationship. This action, which I repeated over and over again, caused me intense untold grief through the years. It is the definition of insanity. Contained within this ominous cloud was the truth that Tom and I had no chance from the very start.

Until I recognized it was me who needed fixing, it was me who needed to make the choices from the opportunities life presented that would build my self-esteem, a healthy relationship would always elude me. Years of living in the shadow would pass before I caught a glimpse of light and fully grasped when I was about to sabotage myself.

~~~~~~~~

After the awkward conversation with Karl, Tom and I went to Rehoboth Beach for some fun in the sun. Just after we spread the blanket on the hot sand and were about to sit in our beach chairs, Karl suddenly appeared from out of nowhere. Both my jaw and heart dropped at once. Feeling like I had my hand caught in the cookie jar, guilt expressed itself throughout my body. The only thing I heard was, "Debbie, how could you?" Without waiting for a reply, he simply walked away.

The confrontation was surreal, and it left me speechless. Even if Karl remained standing before us, his question, now seeming more a statement, could not have been answered. The silence lingered as I glanced at Tom. Unfolding the scene in my mind, I became irritated and then incensed; how did he know we were here? To this day, that answer eludes me.

There was an unusually cool ocean breeze for late July, making it comfortable to be outside. It took a fair amount of time for me to restore my emotions and relax and enjoy the day with Tom. The encounter, however, lingered in my thoughts. Since it took place early in the morning, Karl had to be in town.

The coincidence sent shivers down my spine. I did my best to shake off the uneasy feeling but was unable to until Tom took my hand and led me to the ocean, where the waves broke at our feet. Meandering along the oceanfront, we decided to extend our stroll to the boardwalk.

We passed Dollie's, famous for its salt water taffy and caramel corn. Suddenly, Tom stopped and pointed toward the street sign; it read "Olive Street." Shrugging my shoulders, indicating I didn't understand, he pulled me close, wrapped his arms around me, and said, "Olive you."

Whispering in my ear, "I love you," he then brushed his lips gently against mine, kissing me tenderly. At that moment, the drama of the morning dissipated, and all I could think of was how much I loved him. My heart danced to the rhythm of its beat; I was in heaven.

In truth, it was the beginning of the end.

After filing for divorce, I offered Karl anything we held jointly, even giving him my grandmother's furniture. However, there was one item we argued over: a framed print of Paulina Campanelli's *Raspberries*. I was unclear if it was the picture he wanted or the bickering that held us together. Conceding, I let it go and later purchased another one.

My house seemed to have a revolving door; one day, Karl moved out, and the next day, Tom moved in. These early days were some of the happiest, holding wonderful memories we formed as a couple. There was romance in the air; one evening, we drove to the beach for a Drifters concert.

The atmosphere was sentimental; it reminded me of a perfect date, one you read about in a romance novel: a blanket spread on the grass; a bevy of hors d'oeuvres, including various cheeses, crackers, sweet red grapes; sparkling cider in champagne flutes; and of course, the sound of 1950s music floating through the air.

Another fond memory occurred the following January, when Tom, in his own way, proposed to me. He calmly stated, "We should get married." Although blindsided, I was touched by his offer, as well as taken aback because the ink on my divorce papers was still wet.

Naturally, living as the Addict, powerful emotions took precedence over any hesitations I may have had, as I craved a wonderful life full of love and white picket fences. There was a critical incongruence between my head and heart, leading me always to make unwise choices. The plan was a secret; no one would be privy to it, not even my parents.

The proposal led to a civil ceremony on March 5, 1996, when we eloped to Elkton, Maryland, the quickie wedding capital of the East Coast, to stand in front of a justice of the peace, who officiated. Just as the JP pronounced us husband and wife, I noticed a tear roll down Tom's cheek. Holding a single red rose, I felt tears streaming down my face as well.

Unfortunately, one week to the day, our marital bliss was interrupted before it began, as an accident took its toll on us, more specifically, on me. I was driving home from a direct sales party late one evening when a car ran a stop sign, broadsiding me. The force of the impact was strong enough to push my car over one hundred feet down the road, spinning it 180 degrees, where it finally came to rest facing oncoming traffic.

My head and left elbow struck the driver's window, sending me into a state of shock; I could see stars. Not able to move a muscle, I sat stunned, as my body shook from the violent impact. The effect of the collision was evident by my response to a good Samaritan who approached my window and asked if I could start my car. Unaware of the additional peril that lay before me, I heard myself scream, "What the fuck for?"

Suddenly, a wave of clarity brought me back to the present, realizing I was in the direct line of traffic quickly heading my way. However, fear of another crash paralyzed me. Just as fast, an unknown force commanded me to heed the bystander's words, and I started my car and guided it safely off the highway. Once there, I collapsed, still trembling uncontrollably.

The angel who assisted me returned to my car window and asked if he could call someone for me. Since my parents were only minutes away, he called them first and then notified Tom. My dad was by my side in less than twenty minutes, directing me not to move and explaining that an ambulance was en route. The faint sound of sirens in the distance grew louder as the EMT transport neared.

Tom arrived shortly after I was placed in the ambulance, donning a neck brace to prevent potential injury from occurring. After passing several tests before being discharged, Tom and I finally got home at four in the morning.

~~~~~~~~

Life was irritating. Little annoyances picked at me, as my injuries interfered with our newly wedded status, preventing us from enjoying this phase of our marriage. Upon reflection, it was this pivotal time, the beginning of our life as a married couple, when things began to unravel, and our loving relationship began to erode.

The injuries I sustained were genuine, yet it almost seemed like I was feigning all of my pain. Tasks such as heavy lifting for doing laundry, raising my arms overhead to get a plate from the cabinet, and similar household chores were off-limits. Since I was unable to perform these tasks, they didn't get done, and the feeling of being perceived as weak dominated my thoughts. After all, I was a successful, independent career woman, someone who should be able to work through anything.

Physical therapy, doctor's appointments, medications, and eventual surgery to repair an entrapped ulnar nerve all disrupted our postnuptials, leading to a rocky start even before the public ceremony on September 15. Once more, life became a roller coaster. Some days were smooth; some were not. Here we go again: chaos running amok in my life.

~~~~~~~~

Despite the irritations and annoyances, two absolutely unconditional loves entered our lives. For my fortieth birthday, Tom brought home a midsize box with holes in the top. He set it down and opened it up, and to my delight, out bounced a silver-dappled dachshund, complete with a big red bow.

Growing up, my brother and I both had allergies that prevented our family from having a dog. Despite wheezing, itchy and watery eyes, hives, as well as a lot of sneezing, I loved to pet them. My affinity to dachshunds was a result of Fletcher, a red-headed wiener dog who lived with our neighbors to the right, and Petey, a black and tan one who lived on the left.

I named him Frankie, short for Frank F. Urter. He was born on January 1, 1996, and was four months old. I never had a puppy before, and his playfulness took me back to my childhood. The joy of being in the midst of such innocence took the sting out of the bickering between Tom and me.

One day soon after Frankie's arrival, I found I had hives all over my forearms. Dreading I was still allergic to dogs, I went to the allergist to be tested. Luckily, I had outgrown my childhood sensitivity but was still allergic to grass, which Frankie had come in contact with.

That summer, we rented a small cottage in Rehoboth Beach and went almost every weekend. The majority of our time was spent at Cape Henlopen, a beach allowing vehicles on it, as long as you were fishing; it was also pet-friendly. We would drive the Jeep onto the beach, place a fishing pole down by the ocean, and best of all, let Frankie play in the sand.

It was the beginning of August when I saw an ad in the paper for a dachshund-Chihuahua mix. I wanted this little puppy as a friend for Frankie, but Tom was hesitant. He quickly changed his attitude, however, when we went to the home and were presented this tiny puppy, weighing only two pounds and covered in fleas. We needed to save this pathetic thing. So we handed the owner ninety dollars and brought her home.

We named her Chessie. Well, I named her Chessie, short for Francesca. Indeed, she did weigh only two pounds and fit nicely in the pocket of my robe. I was captivated with this little creature who, despite her size, had a big personality. In addition, her maternal instinct was evident by her mothering of Frankie, who was a few months older but also still a puppy. They were perfect together and never seemed to growl at each other, unlike their human parents.

Our wedding was just around the corner, and my parents had given us the nod they would puppy-sit. My heart broke at the thought of leaving them. Unbeknownst to me, my heart would be broken in a few short years.

CHAPTER 12

The Honeymoon Phase

"That honeymoon phase is so much fun in real life when you meet and discover somebody new and fall in love and chase them. The pursuit. And that climactic final moment of ultimate togetherness."
~ Lucas Neff ~

It was a beautiful Sunday in September; nary a cloud was in the sky as I stepped onto the porch in a sleeveless fitted gown, covered from top to bottom with beading. The train was plain white satin to offset the dress's embellishment; the lace armbands had accentuating beads, as did the headpiece.

Feeling like a princess, I swooned for the photographer as Tom opened the limousine door for me. We were headed to the Concord Country Club, just over the Pennsylvania state line, for our wedding ceremony and reception. When we arrived at the country club, the photographer wasn't there. Where was he? He couldn't have gotten lost.

The princess was starting to morph into a witch as a small knot inched closer to my throat when the concierge sent me a note from the photographer; he had run out of gas and would arrive shortly. This innocuous action opened the floodgates of gloom for me.

Pulling myself together to walk down the aisle, I ignored the anxiety spreading through my body. The atmosphere felt like being in the middle of a Hatfield and McCoy battle; it was energetic in nature, and I needed to cool down.

However, the day only worsened as I began to fear deep down our marriage was predestined for failure. Letting go of that thought, I focused on the room itself; although elegant, it was too spacious for the limited number of guests, which left the acoustics from the band echoing off the walls. The ensemble, with a top-notch reputation, now sounded like a high school marching band.

It only got worse.

My resentment grew when Tom mentioned at the last minute his business partner wasn't coming, preferring to spend the day at an Eagles football game. Indignation further complicated my emotions when a colleague of mine handed me an unwrapped Christmas tree skirt as our wedding present; she had also not bothered to tell me her husband wasn't attending. I began to bristle.

The last straw was when Tom avoided me during our entire reception, preferring to mingle with his family instead of with the other guests and me. So when the time came to cut the cake and feed it to each other, I felt justified smashing it into his face, icing and all. Apathy set in, alleviating the anger, but I knew this was not how to start a marriage.

Several archetypes were vying for attention; again, popping up like the whack-a-mole game. Was it the Invisible Child who needed to be seen, or was it the Victim who needed to let everyone see how unfairly they were treating me? Was it both, or another one altogether? Thoroughly entrenched with the idea of having the perfect wedding, I was fixated totally on myself, unaware of the effect on others. My sense of entitlement dominated the occasion.

As a dry drunk, my character defects magnified: "Look at what everyone is doing to me. Poor me. Poor me. Pour me another drink." I was taking everything personally, holding on to all the resentments, replaying them over again in my head. As a result, greater pain ensued, while the objects of my anger were unaware I gave my power away to them.

Silently, I prayed for a miracle.

Afterward, Tom apologized for ignoring me, so we kissed and made up. It was a blessing because I was eager for our honeymoon; we were staying at the Frenchman's Reef Marriott on the island of St. Thomas. Childlike anticipation filled me with giddiness, as we readied to leave.

Since it was the middle of September, the height of hurricane season in the Virgin Islands, we found a fabulous rate on our hotel. Despite the high probability of torrential downpours and excessive winds, the entire week consisted of abundant sunshine, endless blue skies, and soft trade winds.

The weather was perfect, as was most of our time together. For one of our excursions, we went snorkeling, anchoring at several locations, one more beautiful than the other. Our last dive reef was lined with giant rock formations, tempting a game of hide-and-seek.

We waded into the water, wearing our snorkel apparatus, anxious to see the brightly colored fish darting about as we paddled past them into deeper waters. The various species were awash with brilliant hues, from deep indigos to fluorescent yellows to ruby reds. Connecting in a spiritual sense with this aquatic environment, I was in awe of God's amazing world.

Lost in profound reflection, I became separated from Tom. As I glanced to my left, looking for him, I noticed a condensed school of fish retreating hastily. I wondered what set off their sense of urgency, but when I turned the other way, I instantly saw the answer. I froze; time stood still. Fear engulfed me as I came eye to eye with a five-foot-long barracuda.

I pressed myself not to panic and remain calm, and then Tom suddenly appeared from nowhere. Gesturing with his hand, he pointed to the shoreline, indicating the direction to go. Ensuring no sudden movement in the water, I calmly swam to the beach. It was only then that I felt a rush of adrenaline dissipate from my body, as I collapsed in the sand. I knew the barracuda wouldn't bother me if I didn't bother it, but encountering one close up was extremely unnerving. It took several minutes for me to regain my composure.

There were beautiful moments during our honeymoon. On one occasion, we visited St. John's, boarding a ferry to access the island. We arrived at the dock just as it anchored, allowing the locals to disembark: construction workers, schoolchildren in uniform, artisans, and laborers. Each one was more different than the other, but they all had the same destination: St. Thomas.

I briefly looked around and noticed there was no one else on the dock. I realized we were the only two people taking the ferry back to St. John's and wondered to myself, *Where is everyone?* When we arrived, the answer became apparent. Being the smallest of the islands, not only is it free of commercial property, but more than half of the island is occupied by a national park. There is nothing to tarnish the pure and pristine natural habitat.

Turquoise water lapped gently onto the white, sandy beach, while soft sea breezes lured the lush palm trees down to the pastel hibiscus and bright bougainvillea. With the aroma of coconut filling the air, paradise was complete.

As we investigated the various excursions available, a tram car pulled up alongside us. "Would you like a tour of the island?" asked the driver, who said his name was Beaver.

What a strange name, I thought, chuckling to myself and poking Tom in the ribs. "Sure, why not?" I said as we hopped aboard the tram with enough seating for twelve.

Reading my mind from earlier, Tom asked the driver, "Where is everyone?"

"It's hurricane season," Beaver replied, "and the island is deserted." Excited we had a personal tour guide, we found Beaver to be quite the conversationalist. In fact, he loved to talk. He drove us around the national park, stopping at idyllic sites to take photographs while endearing us with elaborate tales of his adventures.

He stopped at an unusual spot: a large tree containing a swarm of honeybees that had built a giant honeycomb in a hollow. It was a unique sight. After getting a good buzz, Beaver delivered us to Cinnamon Bay, a mile-long beach within the park, saying he would return in four hours for the trip back to the ferry. You couldn't ask for more; everything was falling into place.

After unloading our bags from the tram, we bid adieu to Beaver and walked toward the beach. After scoping it out, we instantly looked at each other as if having the same thought. It was very odd; the day was perfect, the sun was shining, and though the temperature was over 90 degrees, the cool breeze made it delightful to be outside.

What was strange was that the beach was vacant; besides the two of us, no one else was present. Cinnamon Bay was one of the most famous and romantic beaches in the Virgin Islands. After I spread my beach towel on the sand, I casually strolled to the water's edge and allowed my mind to wander. I was in love, and we had the entire beach to ourselves; it was the perfect honeymoon spot.

The warm seawater splashed my feet; it felt pleasant, and I found myself wading deeper until it was waist-high. I looked down, amazed that the water was so crystal-clear I could see the red polish on my toes. In my heart, I wished time would stand still so this moment could last forever.

Taking a walk along the beach, we discovered only one other person: the owner of the little bamboo Tiki Hut who rented snorkel, surfing, and other water sports equipment. He seemed to read our thoughts as he nodded: *Yes, hurricane season is bad for business, but a day like today, well, it was perfect for a honeymoon.*

CHAPTER 13

My Dark Night of the Soul

There can be no rebirth without a dark night of the soul,
a total annihilation of all that you believed in
and thought that you were.
~ Hazrat Inayat Khan ~

The honeymoon phase was over, and we settled into our lives with mundane routines. Where did our love go? Before getting married, I was the center of Tom's attention; he sacrificed other areas of his life for me---rearranging his work schedule, forfeiting his daily run, and spending less time with family and friends. The feelings that were intoxicating when our relationship changed from friends to lovers, however, vanished.

He used to call frequently just to hear my voice, sent roses, left daily cards expressing his affection; the list was endless. The shower of love letters, sentimental trinkets, romantic dinners, and enchanting walks in the park holding hands were now a distant memory. Even my pet name, Kitten, was absent from his vocabulary.

It was like a light switched turned on and then off; one day, it seemed all my dreams had come true, and the next day, I woke up with my bubble burst. Oh, how I yearned to turn back the clock to the hour we couldn't let each other go, living in the now of us, those precious days where it felt like we were walking on sunshine.

~~~~~~~~

During the first years of our marriage, there were happy times sprinkled between the arguments and challenges every couple faces. Not expecting our future to unfold this way, one day I wondered *why* this was happening. What would cause a man to shift gears overnight? The answer suddenly became apparent: the chase was over, he won, and now it was time to focus on another project: building his internet credit-card processing business.

Life with Tom took on new meaning when we agreed to start a family. After several fruitless months of trying to conceive, we decided to seek the help of in vitro fertilization (IVF).

To determine if there was a problem with me getting pregnant, my OB/GYN scheduled a few tests. The first one was a laparoscopy, where an incision was made near my navel, and a laparoscope, a thin device, is inserted to see if endometrial tissue was growing outside of the uterus. It was; I had endometriosis.

After the doctor removed as many of the lesions as he could, the next step was to see if I had any blockage in my fallopian tubes. The procedure, a hysterosalpingogram, was a painful type of X-ray, where a contrast agent or dye is injected so the uterus and fallopian tubes are visible.

The result showed no blockage, which dashed my hopes of a natural pregnancy. It was now apparent we had to take the IVF route to conceive, which was an expensive, emotional, and time-consuming proposition. Before we started the process, I underwent two additional laparoscopies, the last being the most severe.

My left fallopian tube was attached to my bowel, and there was a chance it could be perforated. As a precautionary measure,

I was ordered to cleanse my colon by changing my diet and drinking a gallon of water mixed with magnesium citrate.

It was an outpatient procedure, and I could go home shortly after I came out of recovery. Unfortunately, a complication ensued that afternoon: my stomach became overly distended, causing painful cramps. Unable to have a BM, I returned to the doctor's office for a suppository, and when it was ineffective, I had to be admitted to the hospital for monitoring.

I felt alone in the hospital, and depression overcame me. An IV drip, releasing Dilaudid every four hours, was put in my arm. I also had a catheter inserted, and I wasn't sure why because I could urinate. All I could do is just lie there, playing the victim, feeling sorry for myself.

After dinner and visiting hours were over, I wallowed deeper in self-pity; my husband didn't come to visit, nor did he even call to see how I was. My mind created scenarios of why he wasn't with me; most of them only led me to a darker place where isolation, abandonment, anger, fear, and sadness dwelt. Although not in physical pain, due to the Dilaudid, my emotional pain was crushing. Where was my loving and faithful husband?

Finally drifting off to sleep, it was past eleven o'clock when something woke me up. It was Tom, sweet-talking the overnight nurse at her station and attempting to contrive five minutes to slip in and visit with me quietly.

He apologized for not coming sooner, adding, "I have a surprise for you." He took a package from behind his back and handed it to me, adding gleefully, "I brought you my dessert from dinner: cheesecake."

My stomach churned at the thought of it. Liquids were on the menu for me this evening, so I was unaware plain cheesecake is on the list of acceptable sweets and viewed this act of kindness as being disingenuous. Amplified by the narcotics, the Victim fully cast its shadow.

I looked visibly let down and directed my frustration at Tom.

I snapped, "Are you serious? Cheesecake?"

The Victim, and the ungrateful bitch in me, swung hard and fast; their cries demanded sympathy. My inappropriate actions usually put me into emotional turmoil, where I gave my power away, and the more I gave away, the stronger my resentment grew.

We managed to stay the course, taking the next step for IVF. Since endometriosis may be a cause of infertility, it was suggested I complete a three-month round of Lupron Depot to help stimulate the production of estrogen, helping to ensure that it was successful.

There were side effects, however, which pulled my emotions from one end to the other. I found stopping at a red light would cause me to cry maniacally. When I went to get my injection and the Band-Aid was put on by someone other than my regular nurse, tears rolled down my face. I was losing control of my emotions.

Going through these months to prepare for IVF was like riding a never-ending roller coaster; I felt I could no longer continue with the process. As much as I'd have loved to have had a Little Debbie running around, I didn't feel it was necessary to give birth to a child to be a mother.

After discussing IVF's psychological impact on me, we decided to adopt a little girl from China with the help of Adoptions from the Heart. The organization was highly successful in placing foreign children in permanent homes, so we attended a meeting to learn more about it. Everything was unfolding smoothly, and I was excited at the thought of adopting a baby girl.

My excitement was short-lived, however, when Tom informed me he no longer wanted children. I was stunned and asked why he changed his mind. He didn't give an explanation, which only left me in a state of confusion.

His change of heart had nothing to do with me; I know that now. What left me downcast was being left in the dark, wondering what was happening. Something was wrong, but I couldn't quite put my finger on it.

Heartbroken at the realization I would remain childless (I don't have the Mother archetype), another disappointing experience occurred on my birthday, which placed a wedge between us. Tom arrived home from a business trip well past one o'clock in the morning and woke me from a sound sleep so that he could give me my present.

He told me, "You're going to either love it or hate it."

I was still foggy but awake enough to be put off by his remark, thinking, *What a terrible thing to say about the birthday gift you're giving*. It was wrapped in a large box with the paper falling off. I recognized the name of the store; I had seen it in an airport when I traveled with him once.

Feeling this was just an obligatory gesture with no emotional attachment, I opened the box, not fully awake. The item inside looked like a purse, but I wasn't sure. It slowly dawned on me: it was a backpack. *A backpack?* Well, it was a Dooney & Bourke, after all.

"Look," Tom said, proudly directing my attention to the medallion hanging off the rear flap. "I had it engraved for you with your initials." I hated it. I hated it as much as I hated that he made business plans for my birthday, and I hated it as much as the fact he left immediately after his gift-giving ceremony for another business trip. I felt abandoned and alone.

Trying to process the rationale of my husband's two-hour visit increased my persistent gnawing that something wasn't right. My intuition that our marriage was in trouble kept trying to break through the surface, but I was in denial. If the saying "Denial ain't a river in Egypt" was true, then I was the queen of denial.

The Saboteur's shadow had a viselike grip on me. I was unaware that my response to what was happening in my life — that everything was normal — was the result of my projections from my personal experiences. I was looking at the world through a set of filters that prevented me from seeing things as they were. To say it plainly, I wasn't strong enough to see the truth. As a result, I made a choice to do nothing, blocking my empowerment, and not taking responsibility for myself.

For the next eight months, I seesawed between wanting to save the marriage and ending it. Confliction was my norm, so I decided to work on myself — reading books on personal growth, praying, journaling, asking questions — to see if it would help. The results were mixed; for me, the outcome was positive, but it only further tore us apart. For some reason, Tom didn't like that I was trying to better myself. I can only speculate that it was his issue and had nothing to do with me.

I suggested to Tom that we go for marital counseling, even opting for a male therapist in order to not have the appearance of two females joining forces against him. And although he agreed to go, it was begrudgingly. During one of the sessions, I became acutely aware of just how powerful the word *probably* is. When the counselor asked my husband if he punished me by withholding love, he answered, "Probably." Probably? In my opinion, he did withhold love from me.

It was during this tumultuous phase of our marriage when I realized that, despite the fact I was repeating the same behavior patterns as before (falling in love with the idea of being in love), there was a difference this time. One distinction for wanting to save the marriage was financial. The Prostitute, who never remained dormant, viciously increased its presence. Caroline Myss writes, "The Prostitute archetype engages lessons in the sale or negotiation of one's integrity or spirit due to fears of physical survival or for financial gain." In no uncertain terms, this was my situation.

The truth is, I stayed in the relationship for as long as I did, not so much because I wanted it to work, but because I needed to survive in the physical world. One of my biggest fears, financial insecurity, was that I couldn't afford the mortgage on the house by myself. Once more, I was given an opportunity to develop inner self-esteem and failed miserably, allowing the shadow of the Prostitute to hold me captive.

The other fear that kept me from walking away was the fear of being alone or not seen. "The Invisible Child archetype," according to Myss, "is the child that wasn't acknowledged, and not being seen was very painful." She adds, "The shadow aspect manifests as someone who creates drama and makes a scene in order to be noticed." There were plenty of arguments, as well as my attempts to get Tom to see me when I needed him to.

One argument centered around my going out dancing. Tom was upset when I came home late, asking who I danced with. I was with my girlfriends, listening to great music, and having fun, but he didn't believe me. In reality, I never did anything wrong, but I questioned myself, asking why else did I go? Truthfully, I acknowledged it was the attention I craved, since I didn't receive it at home.

As I mulled over the reason Tom would be suspicious of me going out, I remembered when we first met, and he would join me at Westminster House for ACOA meetings. Having shared the intimate reflections I had about Mark then, perhaps he believed I was now acting out on my thoughts.

My life was spinning out of control; I was on an emotional roller coaster that was going to crash. One day I would say, "This is the last time I will ever shed tears over Tom. It's over," and the next day, "Maybe we can work this out." It went on for almost a year; I was sick and tired of being sick and tired, but I could not be the one to walk away.

It seemed ironic that when I finally came to accept the marriage was ending and began to withdraw emotionally; Tom did an about-face. He told me he wanted to work on the relationship, especially when we went to Aruba, an incentive trip I earned with my company.

~~~~~~~~

The trip to Aruba was like another honeymoon, and we had a great time, the best in years. It was fun and adventurous and felt like the old days. We enjoyed several excursions, romantic dinners, and intimate evenings.

It seemed like the clock turned back; Tom's attitude toward me was kind, generous, and very loving. Any thoughts of divorce slipped away when he purchased a stunning seventeen-carat tanzanite-diamond bracelet for me. Although I felt it was too expensive, he disagreed.

Tom had arranged a few meetings on the island for work, but I didn't care. He was the man I fell in love with, and I was in heaven. Aruba gave me a new lease on life and new hopes for our marriage. It was only temporary, however, as a decision was about to be made that would send me into the dark night of the soul.

When we returned home, life reverted back to what it was, only worse. We argued about everything, including my upcoming surgery. Two days after the procedure, he sent a limo driver to take me for my follow-up appointment; he said he was too busy. Within two weeks, and just over a month from our trip to Aruba, Tom announced he was filing for divorce.

Panic raced throughout my body, and the fear of uncertainty took hold. Everything in my life felt like it was slipping away; I was slipping away. The knot at the end of the rope had unraveled, and I could feel myself falling deeper into despair. Although I cried, begged, and pleaded for him to reconsider, he would not. The pain of rejection ripped through my heart; I felt it being torn apart, bit by bit, into tiny little pieces.

Pitifully, I whined, "What did I do?"

Still not wanting to believe my husband was filing for divorce, I did everything in my power to stop him. My last act of desperation resulted in a humiliating and pathetic scene, one which still breaks my heart. We were sitting on the sofa when his demeanor shifted from casual to stern. The energy in the air was acute; I knew the decision he made was firm. As Tom stood to leave the room, I fell to my knees, grabbed one of his pant legs and wailed, "You promised you'd *never* abandon me."

He continued to walk away, dragging me for several steps, until I let go and unceremoniously fell into a heap on the floor. Everything seemed to squeeze out of me. The entire world I created in my mind ceased to exist, shattering, leaving me an empty shell of a person, physically present but void inside.

I was entering the dark night of the soul, where nothing made sense anymore, and there wasn't any purpose. My identity and sense of security was shaped around my marriage, and if my marriage ended, I ended. What really was falling apart was the whole conceptual framework for my life, the meaning I had given it, which left me in a dark place.

When in the dark night, there is the possibility of emerging out of it into a transformed state of consciousness. Life has meaning again, but it's abstract, without a meaning you can explain. Often it's from here that people awaken out of their conceptual sense of reality, which has collapsed, into a deeper sense of purpose that cannot be defined.

The dark night of the soul is a type of death that you die, an egoic death. What has died is your illusory identity. You now recognize at a soul level, rather than a conscious one, that you are connected to all that is. This is often part of the process of spiritual awakening.

I didn't know just how dark it would get.

CHAPTER 14

Hitting Rock Bottom

*Sometimes God lets you hit rock bottom so that you
will discover that He is the rock at the bottom.*
~ Dr. Tony Evans ~

My marriage was over. The realization was unbearable, and it felt like I was dying. It was at this moment, the very thought of dying, when I forced the paralyzing feelings of abandonment and rejection down, bottled them up, and returned to the "*look good*" little girl I knew so well. Denying the loss of what little self-esteem I built in the past years, I began a quest to have a little fun and pursue someone who would give me what I couldn't give myself: love.

I was only delaying the inevitable.

~~~~~~~~

When out one Saturday night dancing to a popular band, my attention focused on a man I frequently saw. I approached him and introduced myself. I was very attracted to him and could feel a sexual overtone slowly building, and as it grew, my excitement heightened as well.

Since I was still legally married and hadn't felt this way for a long time, there was a strong feeling of taboo. Thoughts of Andy swirled in my mind, creating a disastrous concoction of fantasies that would ultimately lead me down a path of destruction, crossing a line I swore I never would when I first quit drinking. I told myself I would *never* drink again.

That all changed the evening I offered to bring him a baked ziti dinner. When I arrived at Andy's house, he had set the table, complete, down to the wine glasses. When I saw them, the thought entered my mind: *One glass of wine wouldn't hurt me*. The battle lines of good and evil lie before me. The pull of the Addict, however, proved to be too tenacious, enticing me with, "It's just one glass. You'll be okay. You're stronger than before." A single sip was all it took, and the consequence of that one decision led me down the path where I hit my rock bottom.

After we finished eating, I felt an innate sense of strength, as for the first time in my life, I didn't want or need a second drink. In the Big Book of Alcoholics Anonymous it says, "Remember that we deal with alcohol — cunning, baffling, powerful!" I found this to be true because the next day, I was thinking about having a drink. Social drinkers don't do that. They also don't plan their lives around alcohol, but I was no social drinker. For the next nine ravaging months, I was incapable of putting down the bottle.

Soon, I determined Andy was like many others I had relationships with; he never complimented me let alone expressed any whispers of love. I allowed him to take advantage of me financially, as well as sexually, and I later discovered he was seeing another woman. Having not an ounce of dignity left, I idealized him as the man of my dreams, when in fact, he was just a lothario.

My life was in turmoil; Tom was still living in my house and about to file for divorce. The bickering between us was a psychological game of tug-of-war that drained me, which initiated my impulsive need to be loved, validated, and seen.

The urge to fill the vacuum within influenced my impulsive choices, giving too much of my attention, my finances, and my physical body to this Don Juan. Resentment for not being reimbursed began to root, much like weeds in a drought. Believing I had changed, the shadow tightly held on, preventing any sliver of light to shine that allowed me to comprehend the meaning of balance.

It wasn't until years later when Dr. Wayne Dyer, one of my favorite spiritual teachers, explained about giving too much too soon: "You start out on an even level; the scales are balanced." He continued, "When one person keeps giving and giving, the other person feels so heavily indebted, they either can't or don't want to give it back, returning the relationship to a more even level. In fact, they feel so weighed down, they flee, running for their lives."

The urge to bang my head against a brick wall remained; my ongoing pursuit to control situations only saw them backfire. After several months of chaotic living, I threw in the towel; two's company and three's a crowd. I vowed never to call or see Andy again; I was done with his game-playing. Once more, any thread of life force I had remaining was knocked out, leaving me crumpled into a little ball of nothingness.

The Addict was more devious and conniving than ever. That one glass of wine turned into two, and within two weeks, I was drinking a bottle of Kendall Jackson Chardonnay daily. It was expensive, so I lowered my standards by purchasing boxes of wine instead. It didn't have the same bouquet of aroma or the same fruity taste, but it achieved the necessary result.

The partying continued, and I rarely stayed home, in search of anything to fill the void still churning within me. The

Femme Fatale archetype, aroused earlier, now was fully on the hunt. Knowing that my physicality and sensual clothing style enticed men like bees to honey, I set out to conquer. Dressing in an outfit that screamed, "Look at me," for an evening at Delaware's Most Eligible Bachelors event, I was fully prepared. Several attractive men were dancing to my favorite party band, and I won the attention of one of them: a handsome ex-professional athlete.

Over the next several weeks, we shared time together, and I was smitten. I kept my drinking in check, as I didn't want to damage the relationship I thought we had. Once again, life with him and the white picket fence occupied my mind, only to be shattered into a million pieces when I saw him one night with another woman. The dagger plunged deep into my heart, making it difficult, if not impossible, to breathe; I felt humiliated and sunk deeper into the mire.

What appeared to me as an act of betrayal was a breaking point. Making a quick exit before being seen, I asked God, "What's wrong with me? I'm a nice person, yet I keep getting dumped like a piece of trash." Nothing made sense to me, nothing. My life felt like a conundrum, as impossible to decipher as a cryptic message. The shadow looming over me became darker and heavier.

Matters on the homefront were also distressing; we argued about the usual things: property, alimony, and lawyer fees. However, Tom was generous in other matters. Craving to escape my lousy life, I accepted one of those generous offers and flew to Tampa for Christmas, staying on to celebrate the New Year. Perhaps guilt got the best of him because he also paid my hotel and car rental; he even gave me his credit card with unlimited use.

Just as I was leaving my parents' house for the airport on Christmas Day, Karl, his new wife, and his stepson arrived to visit them: an awkward situation. Karl had maintained a friendly relationship with my mother and father, who he considered his adopted parents, which was fine with me; I harbored no ill-will. Walking out the door, I wished them a happy holiday and was off to the airport.

My mother and dad

Being seated in first class had benefits, I thought, as I sipped my complimentary glass of wine. Luxurious leather seats with additional space was another amenity that made the three-hour flight to Tampa more comfortable. Tasting the crisp, fruity Chardonnay, the emptiness I felt inside continued to throb, aching to be filled. Obliging the need, I ordered a second glass, unaware of the slippery slope that lay ahead. All I knew was that I was in pain, and alcohol helped to alleviate it.

As I checked into the hotel and presented the desk clerk with Tom's credit card, I noticed my diamond tennis bracelet was missing. *Damn it*, I thought. *I must have lost it on the plane.* The alcohol was already beginning to cloud my cognitive abilities.

Several uneventful and lonely nights passed, and my drinking increased. On the fourth day of my vacation, I became acquainted with two men who had also just met. One was a younger, handsome man, while the other was a stocky, balding lawyer. The latter invited us to dinner at Don Shula's Steakhouse later in the evening.

After we met and were seated at the restaurant, the lawyer ordered a hundred-dollar bottle of Cabernet Sauvignon. I was delighted and, tasting the wine, found it was full-bodied and firm, pairing excellently with my filet mignon. The three of us enjoyed two bottles of wine and capped the night off with a snifter of Courvoisier.

The next morning, I awoke clear-headed and made a connection between various types of alcohol; the more expensive it was, the less of a hangover you had. The younger man, Sam, and I had made plans to ring in the new millennium together, so we went to the hotel bar downstairs. After a few drinks, we decided to watch the ball drop in my room.

We made ourselves comfortable before I ordered a bottle of White Star champagne from room service, along with strawberries and whipped cream. The order was quick to arrive, and while lying in bed, I raised my champagne glass and toasted, "White Star on Tom!"

~~~~~~~~

As the New Year unfolded, my dependence on alcohol became evident by my night cravings. I routinely woke up after a few hours of sleep and went downstairs for a shot of vodka, which allowed me to sleep a while longer. I was finding it necessary to drink more alcohol just to maintain a natural state of functioning, but it also led me to lower the bar.

As time passed, I began to gravitate to places that were less than desirable. One night in February, I was about to pull into a parking spot outside Gator's, a local taproom, when a car swooped in and stole it.

I angrily yelled, "You fucking dickhead!"

Entering the establishment, I made my way to the bar. Ordering a drink to settle my outrage, I watched someone circle it, stopping right next to me. He said, "I'm sorry I took your parking space. Let me buy you a beer." I accepted the offer, not wanting to turn down a free drink.

After Jim introduced himself, I made my way to the dance floor and noticed he had followed me. He wasn't my type at all; it was obvious he was from the other side of the tracks: wife beater T-shirt, tattoos, and much younger. After last call, he offered me cocaine, and my ears perked up. The Addict, already in full swing, burst forth with even more powerful cravings.

We went back to my house, and to my surprise, he never left.

~~~~~~~~

The tie that bound me to him was his five-year-old son, little Jimmy. He was so adorable yet forlorn. My heart ached whenever he came over, which was more often than not. I fell in love with this little boy, and in some way, he reminded me of my childhood. Jimmy seemed starved for love and attention, just like I was. He appeared to treasure the time I spent reading to him almost as much as I did.

His father, on the other hand, was not so innocent and knew how to skillfully woo a vulnerable woman. I didn't need

143

Victim tattooed on my forehead; the energy of my low self-esteem said it all. He had my number.

Jim knew how to sweep me off my feet, worming his way into my life, not only with love notes, rose petals, candles, and balloons, but by gaining my trust and repaying money he borrowed. There were many advantages to be with me, including having a comfortable place to live, a girlfriend with money to buy alcohol and cocaine, as well as the obvious physical benefits. Life was good for him.

For me, there was no way out. The sense of being trapped in a closely weaved spider's web resulted from the increasing amount of alcohol I consumed. It also distorted perceptions of my thoughts, actions, and beliefs; I rationalized my maintenance drinking, including the midnight shots, as being more controlled than the times I blacked out.

By the end of March, I was not only drinking in the middle of the night, I was cracking open a sixteen-ounce can of Coors Lite at 7 a.m. Making light of my situation, I pronounced the beer as my "Breakfast of Champions." It was no joke when I found myself racing to the bathroom, kneeling down as I prayed to the porcelain throne, heaving it back up.

After the initial regurgitation, I opened another beer, gulping it down to ease the shakes, only to have it, too, expelled. Thankfully, the third one stayed down. It was a daily ritual to avoid having my body shake like a hula dancer on steroids, but it also caused the pungent odor of alcohol to seep through every pore of my body.

My life centered entirely on how, when, and where I could obtain alcohol. No longer a binge- or problem-drinker, I was entering the crisis stage of dependency. The seventeen-year dry spell didn't vanquish my alcoholism. In fact, it exacerbated it: it was as if I had been drinking twenty-seven years, not seven months. Finding it crucial to down larger quantities of alcohol to maintain some semblance of normalcy, I was nearing my rock bottom. Not only did my spiral downward accelerate, but insanity began to appear.

An incident in mid-May validated my madness. Jim wanted to take Jimmy and Tiffany, his niece, to the beach since it was a beautiful, sunny day. We loaded up the car and safely restrained the children in the back seat. Jim sat behind the wheel since I was drinking my vodka-mixed Gatorade.

We were making great time, due to Jim's lead foot. Without warning, a loud voice jolted me.

He yelled, "Fuck, a cop is on me; I'll go to jail if he pulls me over. Debbie, change seats with me."

Not even considering the consequences, I complied. Switching seats while driving (a felony) is insane, especially at 70 mph.

Trying to maneuver into the driver's seat, I swerved off to the shoulder and back to the right lane as I sat down. After pulling me over on the side of the road, the officer asked why I veered off to the side. Thinking as fast as someone who is impaired could, I told him I dropped my cigarette, praying he wouldn't administer a breathalyzer test.

After forty agonizing minutes, he returned my license and registration, along with a ticket for speeding *and* reckless driving. Signing for the ticket, I was relieved we could be on our way to the beach, without a worry in the world, or that I would receive six points on my driving record along with a hefty increase in my insurance premium.

My daily life was unmanageable; I found it impossible to be responsible for ordinary tasks, such as paying bills. As each invoice arrived in the mail, I subsequently placed it in the "fuck-it" file. Unfortunately, my mortgage company wasn't amenable to this, and I soon found myself in a dire situation: foreclosure.

The issue wasn't money; the issue was I couldn't write a check because of my tremors. The Addict was ingrained, resolute in owning my body, mind, and spirit. It rendered me powerless; I had no control over its shadow. Despair and hopelessness anchored within and pulled me further into depression; it was a psychic weight that kept me harnessed in the chains of bondage.

There was no freedom for me; there is nothing worse than not wanting to drink but having to. After making arrangements with my creditors, I sat down, realizing my life was spinning out of control. The next morning, after downing a beer at eight o'clock, I decided to quit drinking. Within a couple of hours, however, I began to regret my decision, as acute withdrawal symptoms appeared quickly.

First, I became anxious and started to sweat. My hands became clammy; it felt like tiny pins were pricking my skin. Trying to settle myself down, nausea set in, and I began to dry-heave, causing acute pain in my stomach. After four hours, the sweat beaded on my forehead, the pins and needles increased, and with it, a strange sense of itching or burning.

After seven or eight hours had passed, the effects of the withdrawal from alcohol intensified to a point where I had little control over the tremors. Shaking involuntarily, I lay down on the family room floor and began to cry, sobbing, "I'm in deep doo-doo." When I finally realized I was in way over my head, alarm bells whistled.

I couldn't take the pain anymore; the tremors and the feeling of wanting to crawl out of my skin were too much. The Addict's grip overpowered me, and without resolve, I told Jim to go to the liquor store and buy a pint of vodka. He complied; keeping me in an obliviated state was key for him. When he returned, I took the bottle and drank the entire contents like water; I still had the shakes, although the tremor-like seizures subsided.

Of all the times I've faced death, this was the closest I had come; I surely would have died without drinking the vodka. My ignorance of alcoholism, coupled with the inability to think straight, focus, and make decisions, led to fear so entrenched it was impossible for me to move forward in life.

I have no memory of the next two weeks. I hit rock bottom.

CHAPTER 15

I Surrender

Surrender isn't about giving up. It's about letting go. When we surrender to our higher power, the journey begins.
~ Unknown ~

I came to. It was 6:45 a.m. on Monday, June 5, 2000. I found myself at Tony's, a friend who lived in North Wilmington, twenty-five minutes from home. I jumped up and, despite my alcoholic fog, realized the dire consequences of my actions from not only the day before but the previous two weeks. There was a total eclipse of my consciousness, apart from celebrating the end of my toxic dependency over the past four months with Jim by changing the locks on my doors.

Panic set in, and I became acutely aware that I hit my rock bottom; my muddled decisions were having damaging effects on my two dogs, Frankie and Chessie, who were dependent on me for their survival. Not only was I awash with guilt for neglecting them, but anxiety pierced my heart about the condition I left them in for the past twenty-four hours.

What had I done, leaving them alone without food, water, or the ability to relieve themselves outside? What kind of monster was I? These questions permeated my thoughts, alternating with how quickly I could get home to my precious fur-babies.

Hastily grabbing my keys, I flew out the door in a flash. My head pounded; the pain felt like being hit with a sledgehammer. As I jumped in my car, the glare of the sun shining directly in my eyes intensified the throbbing between my temples. The cloudless sky was flooded in an ocean of blue, irritating me, but beautiful to everyone on their way to work.

Still reeling from the effects of alcohol, I sped south on I-95 as fast as I could, without a thought of being stopped by the police, not only for a speeding ticket but a field sobriety test, as well. *My God*, I thought. *What am I doing to myself?* I rocked back and forth, banging my fist on the car's console.

Pulling safely into my driveway, by the grace of God, I threw the car into park and ran inside the house. My heart raced as I held my breath, wondering if my pups were all right. Even when you unconsciously mistreat a dog, they are so loving and forgiving, more so than humans.

They both jumped to my knees and greeted me with their little tails wagging, just like windup toys. Thank goodness they were small dogs; they couldn't knock me down, even in my teetering state. Picking up their bone-dry water bowl, I filled it to the top before I quickly fixed their food.

Opening the refrigerator, I noticed four Coors Lites were left on the shelf. Grabbing one, I cracked it open and took a long, slow gulp. Sitting down, intuition, the voice in my head, warned, *You are in so deep that you'll die if you don't get help*. I felt so powerless; alcohol controlled my life, and I had no clue what to do. I needed help.

And there it was: a moment of clarity, where I felt my consciousness open as the grace of God flowed in. *Help; get help*. I never, ever asked for help before. The belief to never depend on anyone for anything, let alone God, had been ingrained within me. Awash in an expanse of helplessness, a foreign and uncomfortable feeling, a sense of sacredness, inspired me to admit I was powerless over alcohol, and my life had become unmanageable: Step 1 in Alcoholics Anonymous.

Just one cursory glance around my house told the story; it was in deplorable condition and felt like an obstacle course just to get to the kitchen. Not only were items strewn about; you could write your name in the layer of dust covering the furniture, and the carpets were begging to be shampooed and vacuumed.

The most offensive thing was the overwhelming stench, created by the weeks old trash left in the bin, coupled with the waste throughout the house from Frankie and Chessie. I would be a candidate for an episode of *Hoarders* unless I did something soon.

Sitting at the kitchen table, drinking my beer, I contemplated on what to do. All at once, those three little words came out of my mouth: "I need help." They were the hardest ones I'd ever spoken in my life, but it was true; the smell of alcohol permeating my skin, oozing from every pore, reminded me of it. I did need help.

Rummaging through the desk drawers in search of a phone book, I tossed the contents, one by one, onto the floor, adding them to the chaos. Doing this reminded me further about my lack of control and discipline. Finally, I had the object of my pursuit in hand. *Now what?* I thought as I sat there. *Where do I look?*

Entitlement shot to the forefront of my mind; there was no negotiating. I would not check into a state-run institution. I was above that; a U-turn from lowering the bar, I looked through the Yellow Pages under Treatment

Facilities and found MeadowWood, a hospital nearby that had a detoxification program.

My hands quivered as I pressed the numbers to call the hospital. The phone seemed to ring forever until a woman finally answered. After I explained my reason for calling, she told me a bed would be available Friday.

"Friday? Are you kidding?"

It was Monday, and I needed help now, today. If I had to wait until Friday for treatment, I knew I'd be dead.

Lingering by the phone, I contemplated calling my mother, whose brother, Father Bill, had helped me earlier with Breakthrough. The lifetime experiences of guilt, shame, and fear inundated me as I deliberated how to tell Mommy about using alcohol and drugs after seventeen years of abstinence.

Just as that dilemma set in, I gazed at Frankie and Chessie, cruelly reminded of my dereliction of duty with regards to them. The image indicated just how incapacitated I had become, urging me to pick up the phone and call. I told myself it wasn't about me, yet it was all about me.

That observation would soon become clear.

By the time I garnered the courage to call my mother, it was 9:30 a.m., and she had been at work for thirty minutes. Finishing the last of my second beer, I cradled the phone to my ear and slowly began to dial her work number. I was tempted to hang up when she answered but didn't. There was a force greater than me at work here. Besides, I had already made the decision to ask for help; now it was time for my body to follow.

I heard myself say, "Hi Mommy, it's Debbie," and felt the tears as they rolled down my cheeks. Nervously slurring my words, I confessed, "Mommy, I have something to tell you. I've been drinking, smoking cigarettes and pot, and doing cocaine. I need help."

There; it was out. Instantly, the weight of the past nine months lifted off my shoulders, initiating a massive sigh of relief within me. I didn't need to control anything anymore; it was in someone else's hands.

I waved the white flag in surrender.

It was no surprise that my mother was stunned, nor that she was at a loss for words on how to reply to my startling and unexpected confession. She could only stammer, faltering in her speech, that she would call Father Bill for his advice. She seemed more anxious than me.

Fear completely engulfed my body, leaving me paralyzed; I was afraid to do nothing, as much as I was afraid to do anything. All I wanted to do was hide and not come out, longing to be that Invisible Child now. After closing all the curtains and blinds, that's just what I did.

I climbed the stairs, crawled into bed, pulled the covers over my head, and began to weep. A tug-of-war ensued; on one hand, I became keenly aware of the burden about to be lifted from my soul, yet on the other, I sensed the tug of the black hole in the pit of my stomach.

My dogs seemed to sense my apprehension and nuzzled under my chin. Their cold, wet noses attracted my attention, and glancing through teary eyes, I saw Frankie looking up at me. One simple act from a loving, faithful companion put me at ease. I would be okay; I had to be. Unconditional love can bring you through the most troubling times of life, and for the first time in a long while, a smile came to my face.

A few hours had passed, and I was still in bed, drinking my last beer, when a knock on the front door startled me. The dogs, barking frantically, jumped off the bed and ran down the steps. It was my parents; not wanting to face them, I refused to answer the door but knew they weren't going to leave.

The doorbell rang incessantly, and the dogs continued to bark. "Go away," I muttered under my breath. No sooner had I said this than my intuition nudged me, saying, *You have to face this; if you don't allow someone to help you, you will surely die.* This idea was not at all appealing; in truth, I did not want to die.

Pushing my ego aside, I reluctantly went down the stairs and sheepishly opened the door. As my parents stepped into the house, all my past failures rose to the surface, leading me to hang my head like a child who just got caught misbehaving. The guilty emotions I had were beyond comparison, and I was unable to look them in their eyes, until my mother told me she spoke with Father Bill. With this news, hope began to chip away at the low opinion I had of myself.

Father Bill laid the groundwork for my admission to Caron after my mother initially called him, ensuring a bed for me. Being related to someone with official duties had its advantages; his actions would save my life, leaving me eternally grateful.

Admittance to Caron required providing proof of health insurance, as well as a driver's license. I looked around for my purse, but it was nowhere in sight. My brow furrowed in panic, as I tried to remember what the alcohol caused me to forget: *Where is my purse? Think, Debbie, think.*

I sat down, trying to recall where I left it, when a memory shot through the haze surrounding my head: I ran out of Tony's house in such a rush, I left only holding my keys. Another conscience-stricken knife plunged into my heart as I gave my dad his phone number, so he could arrange to pick up the pocketbook I left behind. To say I was a letdown to my parents would be an understatement.

By this time, over an hour had passed since drinking my last beer, and my body began to tremble and shake: signs I was withdrawing. To keep them under control, Father Bill instructed my parents to keep me drinking until I arrived at Caron, so my father said he'd stop at the liquor store on the way home from Tony's.

Meanwhile, my mother helped me pack a suitcase for the twenty-eight-day stay. Still reeling under the influence of alcohol, I was incoherent and didn't realize the gravity of my situation. Hearing myself mumble the words, "I'm only going for two weeks because I have bills to pay and business to close," gave me the signal to move forward with the process.

The real reason for resisting the recommended length of treatment was that I couldn't hold a pen steady to write a check to pay my creditors. The mortgage company had given me three days to make payment arrangements before they started foreclosure proceedings, and my utility bills were six months in arrears. My life *was* unmanageable.

Confiding in my mother would reveal my failure to be responsible. But it was true; I had a total disregard for the responsibilities of being a homeowner and also as a human being, placing anything I didn't want to face in the fuck-it file. A cloud of denial wrapped around and protected me; if I didn't see it, it didn't exist.

Immediately upon my dad's return with my purse and Coors Lite, I grabbed a beer, popped the tab, and took a hefty gulp. Despite Father Bill's caution for me to keep the flow of alcohol going, neither my parents nor I were aware the percentage of alcohol in beer was not high enough to prevent the tremors, and I was shaking terribly.

With my suitcase packed, it was time to leave. My mother sensed my hesitation, and with her soft, almost inaudible voice, she assured me that if there was anything else I needed, they would bring it to me. We hopped in the car and began the hour-and-thirty-minute drive to Magic Mountain, Caron's unofficial nickname, derived from being built on Native American burial grounds.

Seated behind the driver's seat, I systematically took one sip after another, while squeezing the six-pack between my feet on the car floor, as if safeguarding it with my life. My mother and I sat quietly while my dad chattered nervously. The phone ringing interrupted him, and he answered the call; it was Father Bill, asking about our status.

My father described my growing tremors, so he suggested we stop at the Black Horse Tavern, located near the facility, for something stronger to drink. We pulled in the parking lot several minutes later, and as my father opened my door, he guided me by the elbow into the tavern and straight to the bar, where he ordered a rum and Coke.

Putting the tiny straw between my lips, I began to sip, not stopping until the glass was empty. Angrily, I spouted off for everyone nearby to hear, "There's no alcohol in this!" But there was; in fact, it was a double. Poor Daddy, He was upset, and now he had to watch me, his little girl, as I became more and more belligerent to customers. His heart must have been breaking. Just as we were leaving, my father needlessly let the bartender know, "It's okay, I'm taking her to rehab."

During Father Bill's previous call, he let me know if I needed additional alcohol after stopping at the tavern, he had some vodka for me. We arrived at the front entrance of the detox building, and I saw him standing there empty-handed. I threw a temper tantrum and yelled, "You don't have any vodka!"

He said, "Of course I don't have any vodka. This is a rehab facility."

"You lied to me!" I cried. "Priests don't lie!"

If this weren't a matter of life and death, the scene that followed would have been comical, and today, I can laugh at it. I walked into admissions with Father Bill holding me up under my left arm, while my dad supported my right side. Since it was medication time, the patients were waiting in line for their prescriptions. Shuffling past them, I waved my hand in the air, declaring, "Hi everyone. I'm here!" Passing a tall individual with wild, gray hair that stood straight up in the air, I commented, "Nice hair, dude." Later, I learned his name was Kai; unfortunately, he died a few weeks later as a result of drinking paint thinner.

There, but for the grace of God, go I.

CHAPTER 16

Spiritual Awakening
and Rebirth

*That is the real spiritual awakening, when something emerges from
within you that is deeper than who you thought you were. So, the
person is still there, but one could almost say that something more
powerful shines through the person.*

~ Eckhart Tolle ~

The nurse began to sign me in, so I said a tearful farewell
to my dad and Father Bill (my mother chose to wait in the car),
and then she escorted me to the room I would occupy for the next
several days. After I unpacked a few things and was ready for
bed, a PA quietly slipped in to check my vitals and dispense my
medications, which included Valium.

Since the tremors I experienced were above the average
range, the doctor ordered a higher dose than usual for me: twelve
milligrams every four to six hours. The effects of the drug set in,
allowing me to drift off to sleep. Within a few hours, however, I
awoke and shuffled to the porch, a large, screened-in area just off
the admissions entrance of the detox ward. The enclosure was the
designated smoking area, and I lit up a cigarette.

It was surprising to me how many people were up smoking cigarettes at one o'clock in the morning. Seeing my perplexed look, the detox patients began to introduce themselves, putting me to ease. Out of the five people sitting down, there were two women, one who said her name was Liza.

Without hesitation, I garbled, "Yes, and you look just like Liza Minnelli."

Under the influence of alcohol, my cognitive abilities were exceedingly diminished, and she didn't respond to my comment. When I finished my cigarette, I bid everyone a good night and wobbled back to my room.

The process to completely wean you off alcohol safely takes four to five days. My liver enzymes were elevated, all vitamins were depleted from my system, especially B and D, and my kidney levels were off. Even my eyesight was affected, though I thought it was just age. The demon alcohol zoomed in, taking root in my mind, holding my physical body prisoner, and spiritually bankrupting my soul.

My first day without a drink was D-Day, June 6, 2000, and I recall little, thanks to the Valium. One emotion I could not forget was gratitude: I was grateful I didn't *have* to drink. The better part of my time in detox was spent restless in bed; the remainder included constant monitoring of my vitals, taking medications, eating, or smoking cigarettes.

One of the few tasks I remember was to complete a form to assess the area for my treatment: Primary Care or Relapse Prevention. Because the tremors in my hands hadn't subsided, still causing me to be unable to write, John, another patient, offered his assistance.

A systematic plan ensued; he asked me the questions on the form, I answered them, and he wrote the answers down. Neither of us were aware we were violating the confidentiality protocol in place; John became privy to the answers containing my personal information that would determine where they placed me.

On my third day in detox, I didn't rise from the dead, but my arms and legs sure did. Due to my physical condition, the doctor didn't want me to walk on my own yet, so a wheelchair was provided to transport me to the nurse's office for my regular checkup. Even I was startled by my poor state of health; not only were my extremities trembling, but my legs shot straight out, appearing as if I were sitting on a jackhammer. It was no surprise; my BP measured 156/120, which I found difficult to believe, but I knew it was true.

Dear God, I thought, *what have I done to myself?*

~~~~~~~~

Even with the self-blame, gratitude began to emerge from within me with each passing day. I had peace, and I was at peace. The battle with the Addict was over, at least for now; by raising the white flag, I surrendered to this disease and won the war. A long, arduous road lay ahead of me, but I recognized that alcohol had more authority over me than my spirit did.

Fully grasping the true meaning of the paradox "We must surrender to win," I was given a gift: a moment of clarity. The definition of *surrender* is to cease resistance and submit to authority.

In AA's lingo, it means, "Let go and let God." It felt as if the first three steps of their 12-Step program happened in one fell swoop: "I can't. He can. I think I'll let Him." I had hope, and with that came a light at the end of the tunnel.

Besides having hope, I also had a sense of safety, as I was now in the hands of Father Bill and Caron. I turned myself over to them, with the willingness to do the required work that would support my sobriety. He was my hero, the same one who called me Princess as a little girl and a dry drunk as an adult. Becoming lucid allowed me to see the truth for the first time: Father Bill was right; I had been a dry drunk for a long seventeen years.

For that duration, the only thing I did was put down the drink; I didn't change. I was still the same person: critical, judgmental, impatient, full of rage, a ticking time-bomb, hating myself and others; a real joy to be around. A slogan in AA says, "The same person will drink again." It took almost two decades, but I did drink again.

Now, I'm in a position where I can make significant life changes, possibilities God graced me with when he lifted the veil, uncovering the shadow that contained my darkness. By answering my pleas for help, I learned that when I let go, I let God. Every day I made choices, as well as changes within, that would enable me to make my journey to the light a reality.

~~~~~~~~~

Friday, June 9, was my fourth day in detox; it was also my father's birthday, and the best gift I could give him was my sobriety. The tremors were still prevailing, but the next morning, they miraculously dissipated, and I felt well enough to go to the gym and work out.

There were rules I didn't know about; wearing a bright pink wristband screamed *detox*, which meant you weren't allowed in the gym because you were still under medical supervision. No one saw me enter the facility; therefore, no one stopped me. The lack of fallout from it gave me a sense of entitlement. I was untouchable, a person who could do no wrong, a narrative that prevailed throughout my stay.

Entitlement was a challenge to let go of, as well as a matter of contention for me. In Caroline Myss's words, entitlement "will always direct you toward powerlessness, and it encourages you to project expectations on to other people that invariably incur

resentment, either you toward them or a mutual resentment."
Whenever I was in my head, fuming over a resentment, I realized
I was *an asshole in a bad neighborhood* and needed to get out of there
fast.

That afternoon, I was released from detox and escorted to
my room. Walking a distance, we finally reached the last room in
the women's hall. Two neatly covered twin beds occupied the
spacious room, along with an alcove comfortably fitting two
desks. A woman was lying on one of the beds; she introduced
herself as Maureen and said she was being discharged later that
week.

She departed four days later, which left me annoyed about
getting another roommate. After several days passed and no one
checked in, I was elated to have the benefit of a private double
room. It only added to my sense of privilege and lack of empathy,
when I heard there were patients in detox waiting for beds to
open. Was there a reason there wasn't anyone assigned to my
room? I never found out the answer to that question.

The results from the intake form John helped me fill out
were in; those in charge made the incorrect decision to assign me
to Primary Care, a unit divided into males and females, where
rules and regulations were established, but no one ever told me
what they were. A fundamental policy guideline warned patients
who were designated to Primary Care *not* to intermingle with
those in Relapse Prevention. Unaware I was breaking bad, I
strolled down the curving walkway to the wall, the designated
smoking area.

As I lit my cigarette, I caught Father Bill's eye as he neared
from the opposite side. We sat down on the wall to chat, in full
view of the staff. Although my unwitting disregard and
subsequent violation of interaction between the two groups was
apparent to all, no one brought it to my attention. Therefore, no

consequences were administered. The privilege of being Father Bill's niece furthered my sense of entitlement, especially when the news I was here for treatment became known.

Within days, staff corrected the mix-up and placed me in Relapse Prevention. The majority of patients who were in this program attended AA meetings in the past, and although I didn't go to AA (with the exception of that one meeting, as noted on my intake form), and since I didn't drink for an extended period of time, I had indeed relapsed. The revision allowed me to linger at the wall, thus allowing me the same liberties.

The work was about to begin.

~~~~~~~~

An optional ten-minute meditation was scheduled twice daily: one in the early morning and one in the evening, before bed. The instructions were simple: Lay on the floor, with pillows supporting your head, and listen to the soft tones of wooden flutes fill the air. While lying in a calm, relaxed state, something unfamiliar suddenly occurred; I noticed my thoughts suddenly stopped flowing.

In their place, images began to appear; it seemed like a movie was being shown in my mind, and I was the projector. I couldn't figure out what was happening, and it left me confused. The very first picture I observed was an eye, and the only eye I was familiar with at the time was the eye atop the pyramid found on the back of a dollar bill.

It would be years before I had any knowledge of the third eye, or the sixth chakra, the eye of intuition. "The sixth chakra," Anodea Judith states in *Chakra Healing*, "is related to the act of seeing, both physically and intuitively." When healthy, it allows us to see the big picture. The lesson for this chakra, according to Caroline Myss, is "seek only the truth," and this is accomplished through wisdom, its power.

Following the picture of the eye, there were capillary waves, or ripples, the kind that occur after throwing a stone into a lake. The ripples grew outward and then slowly faded away. Even though I couldn't make sense of what was happening, I let go, allowing this mystical process to unfold.

The scene that followed contained an array of faces, but they drifted in and out of my mind's eye, emerging through their various features—ears, eyes, nose—making it feel as if I were hallucinating. A diverse group of unfamiliar, nameless people embodied these images: female, male, black, white, Asian, some with glasses, but all around the age of thirty. Several of them came into focus simultaneously and then disappeared before the next segment began.

The first vision that followed the faces was a setting where I was saddled on a horse and seemed to have a camera strapped to my helmet, situating me directly in the movie. Trotting on the horse through a densely-wooded forest, the sunlight shimmered in and out of the trees, projecting a dance between the rays and the shadows that left me breathless. The panoramic view extended 180 degrees, originating from the front, sweeping right, until both the path I was traveling and the horse's tail were visible.

From there, the movie progressed to the Civil War era, where the Yankees, dressed in blue uniforms, marched south on foot, as well as on horseback. Antiquated rifles balanced on their shoulders at the ready, while the blasts from the cannons, slowly becoming visible, roared in the background.

Immediately following the Civil War reenactment, I stumbled upon a mountainous, barren desert in Afghanistan, where soldiers in camouflage gear were armed with howitzers. The blasts from the heavy artillery reverberated so loudly, it was deafening. Then, in the blink of an eye, I returned to the room where I was lying in the midst of over a dozen of my peers.

When I shared my experience, several of the residents asked what I did to elicit the visions. Since I didn't know, I shrugged my shoulders and asked, "Why? Doesn't everyone see them?" With a resounding no, they urged me to record the visions, making them readily available should I wish to peruse them at a later date. Thankfully, I followed their advice and wrote some of them in my notebook.

The following entries were recorded on the dates specified, starting with June 19, 2000:

> The first thing I saw was an eye, followed by the rippling water. Faces floated in and out, but this time, instead of seeming to be around the age of thirty, they aged and included men in suits and ties. Switching to a tank in Afghanistan, then jeeps, then soldiers walking. The following image was a snowman, then Mary, the Blessed Mother, then Christ on the cross. Aquarian-like bubbles or jellyfish appeared, followed by the Space Shuttle exploding. Next, I went through a slinky-like tunnel with multiple colorful bursts, like fireworks. Lastly, I saw the reflection of the faces in the water, upside down, like Narcissus.

The next day, June 20, I chronicled the images from both the morning and evening meditations:

A.M.

> I started the meditation, again, with the Third Eye, the water rippling, and the faces. Soon a faint outline of the Statue of Liberty came into view, followed by a dandelion puff. I then found myself sitting in a train car on railroad tracks going through tunnels that got deeper and darker. As the train exited the tunnel, it turned into a roller coaster going up and down the hills. The faces reappeared, then vanished, with a new

face in the forefront. There were many vibrant colors. The silver fruit of the dandelion blew away in the wind, as it intensified and blew everywhere. There were waterfalls, then desert, then lightning. Finally, I saw a turkey spread its tail, and I watched as it mutated into a Native American Indian headdress, twice.

P.M.

The Eye of Intuition appeared once more, but this time a kaleidoscope of color exploded, one more brilliant than the other. I next saw an indoor marble pool, where there was a woman, a mermaid, under water. Her long red hair perfectly flowed as she swam, clothed in a purple sequined gown. The end of the pool had no barriers to the ocean, only a glass window on the upper wall. The mermaid swam out into the sea, where she encountered a pod of dolphins swimming and jumping in the air. A whale's tale appeared, then an Egyptian ship from the B.C. era, with boatmen rowing, ending with more kaleidoscopes of color.

There were significant messages contained within these visions. The first of importance was the Third Eye. Simona Rich writes, "When you meditate, your third eye may show itself to you without you even trying." She further states, "When you're getting sucked into the fourth dimension, you may experience your journey as going through a tunnel. When you concentrate on the light at the end of the tunnel, this pushes you forward, and you can visit different worlds in different dimensions."

What this suggests is, by opening your Third Eye, you become more spiritually sensitive, enabling you to *see* more intuitively than just your physical sight. You become in tune with the universe, and as a result, you have a better understanding of who you are and what your life's meaning and purpose are. Although I received many gifts during my stay in rehab, this was by far the greatest.

The insight I received from the soldiers from the Civil War and Afghanistan was that they were symbolic of my support group, assisting me with my battle against alcohol. There were additional signs with significant meaning. One was the image of the Statue of Liberty; the gate of freedom for all immigrants entering the United States. It is the symbol of freedom, my freedom from alcohol. The dandelion puff was another example, as the silver fruits, liberated when blown by the wind, floated away freely, landing randomly to sow new seeds.

The roller-coaster image mirrored life before entering treatment: a series of highs and lows, with the lows outnumbering the highs. The mermaid also delivered a message of independence, swimming out of the infinity pool into the sea, toward the dolphins. With no bonds to constrict their movement, dolphins can live independently, just as I could do now, without having to be tied to the bottle; having alcohol available was a prerequisite to any situation I was in.

The visions were like movies, unfolding sequences in my mind, impossible to prevent (not that I wanted to stop them from happening, of course). They continued throughout my entire stay but always opened in the same progression: the third eye, the rippling water, emerging faces that faded away.

After being enrolled in the newly formed Integrated Recovery Program, similar to Breakthrough, the one I went through five years before, the shifting visions of the faces took on the unmistakable appearance of drama masks used for the Muses of comedy and tragedy. They continued to conceal the faces over the following days, but one morning, they slowly slipped away in my vision. Oblivious to the significance this unveiling portrayed, my world was about to be rocked by a sudden, life-altering epiphany.

That meditation is described in the following excerpt:

> The Third Eye opened the "movie," while the ripples in the water followed. The next image, however, was not the faces but curled barbed wire on a fence, similar to what surrounds a prison. From there, the vision shifted to teepees on an Indian reservation, sending visible smoke signals, as an Indian Chief in full headdress ran by. Slowly, the faces with the drama masks came into sight, remaining only long enough to allow the masks to gradually slide off.

Two hours after that meditation, I was required to report to the small group. It was day four of the five-day process of experiential therapy, where a hands-on approach was utilized in role-playing, leading to new insights and self-awareness for each participant.

The intimate group consisted of only eight individuals, and when I was selected to be a participant, my perception of being an elitist was heightened. One of my new friends, Monique, was already in the room when I arrived on that Thursday morning.

As I sat down, Ms. Roberts, the therapist, looked over at me and nodded in my direction; the cue it was my time to share. My raison d'être, aside from the fact Father Bill was the catalyst for all of this, was to question the loss of intimacy in my marriage.

Ms. Roberts challenged me, making it unclear the direction I was to take. She softly encouraged me to return to my childhood, when I was six or seven years of age. Noticing my bewilderment, she prodded, "Just go with it." I followed her directive, asking Monique if she would role-play myself as a little girl.

Monique agreed and sat up, straightening her posture. Unexpectedly, I understood the significance of why the psychologist brought me to this period in my life. It was the time when my mother shut down her feelings and emotions after losing her infant son. It was the time when I began to wear masks. It was the time when I lost my authentic self.

With this realization, I began to speak to Debbie, and during this conversation, it finally dawned on me: many of the wounds in my life were the result of my mother's inability to grieve and cope with *her* loss. By keeping the sorrow and pain bottled up, she wasn't available to her children. Wearing masks was a coping mechanism I employed to cover up the wounds of that unavailability.

To fashion myself into someone who was not just noticed, but big as life, I wore masks, playing various roles that disguised my authentic self. Each one I identified, along with several archetypes, was portrayed by a Kleenex taped to Monique's torso. As I attached the first tissue, I said, "This is the Strong mask, together with the Look Good one." Repeating this gesture, I called out the words, "This is the People Pleaser mask, this is the mask of the Addict, this is the Super Competent one alongside of Perfection, here's the Student's mask, and here's the Athlete's," and so on.

After exhausting the number of masks I could recollect, the therapist had me revisit the situations where I used them to hide, whether it was pretending to be someone I was not, trying to be accepted, or using them to be acknowledged. Since I didn't need to hide or act a certain way for approval anymore, I could remove the masks, bringing back to life the person I was born to be. And so, one by one, I began to peel the covers off. It was during this rite of passage I heard Monique's voice exclaim, "That was your vision this morning. The masks slid away."

Unable to comprehend her words, I needed a moment to gather my thoughts, but when I realized the truth of her statement, goose bumps ran all over my body. Was this real or just a dream? The significance was ethereal, leaving me in a state of awe. Monique was right; the vision from my morning meditation depicted masks melting away, exposing the faces, just as they did in this experience. The counselor, not aware of the visions I had but acutely mindful of my visceral frame of mind, exclaimed, "You've actually had a spiritual awakening."

Having lived in the shadow for so many years, banging my head against a brick wall, it felt like a miracle when God granted me the grace and opportunity to discover my authentic self. In *Sacred Contracts*, Caroline Myss perfectly describes the spiritual awakening, or epiphany, as she terms it, as "a sudden illumination of our intimate union with the divine, where your relationship with God is transformed from one of doubt or fear, into one of deep trust. You suddenly understand that everything in your life has occurred by divine intention, by the grace of God."

I couldn't be more certain at that moment. God had not abandoned me; I had abandoned God. The deeper spiritual truth I gained from this intimate union with God was instantaneous: I didn't believe in God; I *knew* in God because I had conscious contact with the divine. This knowing allowed me to place my trust in something unfathomable, freely and willingly; I knew if I sincerely trusted in God, completing the necessary footwork for whatever it was I was doing, that I would receive everything I needed in life. The positive effect of this spiritual awakening and trust was monumental.

From that moment on, I realized my life was about to change in the way I had been working so resolutely for; just as

Buddha said, "Everything can change in the blink of an eye," it did. A different person emerged from that spiritual awakening. I now understood that change stems from the inside and works its way out.

Although filled with joy and elation, I knew there was a tremendous amount of work to be done, and it came with a price. Having the Seeker archetype as a dominant power within, I was ready to open my soul, go within, and start digging.

CHAPTER 17

The 12 Steps and Beyond

Going beyond simply means taking all we have gained from the steps with us, continuing to utilize these principles in all our affairs, and moving quietly into a greater expansion of those principles we so highly revere.

~ Lynn Grabhorn ~

It was a Monday, the day before the Fourth of July, when I was officially discharged from Caron. My parents arranged to bring me home, and after they expressed how proud they were of me, they said their goodbyes. Unpacking, I began to settle in, feeling proud of myself as well. Frankie and Chessie, my beloved pets, were reunited with me after being taken care of by my parents and Tom, who got them on every other weekend.

I was in a complete state of wonder. The spiritual energy that coursed through my psyche for the past twenty-eight days prompted a 180-degree shift in how I perceived not only myself but the world around me. It felt like the hand of God reached down, bestowed grace upon me, and lifted my veil of darkness, replacing it with a new attitude and outlook on life.

I had the willingness to do whatever was necessary to stay sober. There was a saying in AA that resonated with me: "If you want what we have, you must do what we do." There were no suggestions if you wanted to be a happy, productive person; there were only *musts*. Therefore, it was essential to emulate the people I wanted to follow.

These activities were not always easy, nor what my ego wanted to do. But I knew it was necessary to abide by the guidance of old-timers in order to stay sober and maintain a healthy life. The wounds I suffered over the years far outweighed the challenges, so I continued to heed their advice. My agenda was set: first to check in with an AA member, contact PACE (an addiction facility in Wilmington) and enroll in their after-care program, and finally, go to a meeting.

Even though I resigned to surrender and listen, I occasionally found myself resisting the amount of time the classes would take. I grew defensive when enrolling in PACE, telling them, "But you don't understand; don't you know I have a mortgage and bills to pay?" Soon, though, I found myself easing into a disciplined schedule. PACE was three hours in the morning (Monday, Wednesday, and Friday), and I organized my meetings and work around those times.

Another guideline, or must, they gave me to follow was to attend an AA meeting every day for ninety days; it's called "doing a ninety in ninety." Again, I protested, "But you don't understand. I was out of work for a month and lost my business. I need to rebuild it." Once more, I complied and went to a meeting every day, sometimes two, three, or even four in one day.

~~~~~~~~~

The first meeting I went to, fresh out of rehab, was located in a church called Red Lion. I sat there quietly, and as I heard the words of a stocky man with a white beard, who wore bib overalls without a shirt, my jaw dropped.

He said, "If I could drink safely, I'd be drunk right now. But I can't, and I never could. When I woke up this morning, I was in dry pants and didn't piss my bed. I used to think it was my wife that was unmanageable, but it was my life that was. I consider myself and anyone else in this room, a miracle, who hasn't had a drink today. We're all miracles because I know that all the things that have been done for me, for us, were not humanly possible."

His passionate words stunned me as he spoke. He was so real and down-to-earth; I knew I needed to make this my home group, which is the weekly meeting alcoholics attend, so others get acquainted with them. The jolly, Santa-looking man touched me in ways I'll always remember, especially when he stared directly at me and said, "We know that black hole you have in the pit of your gut because we all had it before we came into AA." Wow, he did know me; he went on, and just as Father Bill said, "Allow us to love you until you learn to love yourself." And I did let them.

He also told me if I worked the twelve steps on that pull-down shade, I would change.

I looked at him and asked, "That's all I have to do to change?"

"It's simple but not easy," he replied.

In my eyes, however, it was straightforward; my endless search for the means to change bore witness to that. It was the key that unlocked my newfound freedom.

It was imperative for me to make the Addict's shadow my ally.

They told me to get a sponsor, another woman, so I got one. They advise getting a sponsor of the same gender, to avoid potential romantic complications; your sponsor walks you through the twelve steps and helps you stay sober. This person is someone you can call anytime when your sobriety is threatened or you need emotional support. A sponsor supports you by staying in regular contact with you and encouraging you to work the program of AA.

They told me to make a coffee commitment, to immerse myself in AA, to attend Big Book studies, to do service work, and to hang out with the winners. I did all of that, knowing that if past behavior is the predictor of future behavior, I needed to conduct myself differently.

I became deeply ingrained in AA's 12-Step program; like a sponge, I soaked up all it had to offer. I couldn't get enough of it; unlike many who stumble in, fearing change, I embraced it. Because I worked the 12-Steps and because I stayed around AA, my life began to change. I began to change. Doors that shut before were now opened. My business grew; within a few weeks, I received a phone call for a replacement part, which magically rolled over into a home show, my first out of rehab.

In my business of direct sales for a leading candle company, I first became a consultant, but after I was offered the opportunity, I became a unit leader. Earning this title included the same responsibility of developing the consultants I sponsored into leaders as well. Your income increased in direct proportion to how many consultants you had under you, as well as how many leaders you promoted. Incentive trips were awarded, as well as other prizes, and I always earned them (with the exception of this past year). A free vacation to the islands was a benefit too good not to achieve.

I had lost my leadership status and pay, but that first show put the wheels in motion for me to set my goals and plan the actions to attain them. Although I didn't receive a bonus that month, I did in August and was promoted to my previous position as leader the following month. Seeing my grit and determination, the regional vice president asked me to give a positive attitude testimonial at the next meeting.

Just as I worked the principles of the program diligently in life, I applied them to business. I spoke about my addiction to alcohol, what happened, and what it was like now. "In AA," I said, "we trust God, clean house, and help others. In our business, we trust God, hold shows, and help others."

At the end of my testimony, I was humbled when everyone stood up, applauding. Several people approached me with tears in their eyes, expressing their gratitude for my words.

How could I not be humbled? My purpose is to serve and help others.

One of the most dramatic changes occurred within me when I yielded to Step 3: "Make a decision to turn our will and our lives over to the care of God as we understand Him." My past experience with the universe was that it revolved around me and what I wanted. Trying to control people, places, and things always failed, leading me to erupt in anger.

By letting go, I allowed members to love me until I learned to love myself. My stinkin' thinkin' needed reprogramming, so I consciously removed these words from my vocabulary: *try, probably, blame,* and *deserve.* I worked the twelve steps tirelessly until I began to live them. Willing to go to any lengths to change, I listened and followed directions.

Before long, I noticed more changes in myself: I was feeling thoughtful, secure, and grateful. I also began to live more in present time; when driving, I let people pass without reacting, not allowing other people's actions to upset or anger me, and most meaningful, remaining independent of what others thought of me. I didn't become attached to the spectacle, the emotion, and let it pass.

It wasn't always easy, nor was my progression in a straight line. There were many times when I regressed, falling back on old thought patterns and behavior. One revolved specifically around the Femme Fatale archetype and a secret I was holding. I heard from members in AA, "You are only as sick as your secrets," and this secret needed to be brought out into my awareness. It would be, but not until more than a decade later, when I was confronted by Caroline Myss during a workshop at the Miraval in Tucson, Arizona.

The hidden issue was related to my lack of healthy self-esteem: not being good enough, as well as not being seen, which caused me to have the need for men to want me. I still had the need to be recognized from the outside, and I wanted men to look at me, find me attractive, and compliment me.

Several months into my sobriety, one of my male friends lectured me, "You're a beautiful woman. I want to smack you for having such low self-esteem."

I didn't understand what he meant until Caroline Myss echoed these words.

~~~~~~~~

The Serenity Prayer is recited at the end of AA meetings, and people always add this slogan: "Keep coming back; it works if you work it." In my early recovery, I held on to that saying like my life depended on it, and it helped me make healthy choices for the first time in my life.

One of those decisions occurred when I came across an acquaintance at an AA clubhouse. After she casually remarked about a situation I was unaware of, my heart stopped. After feeling the blade of an invisible dagger tear through the flesh into my heart, my first reaction was to become enraged. The anger that boiled up inside of me was justifiable, and I wanted to exact revenge at that very moment.

Justifiable anger, I'm told, will kill you.

Everything now made sense. Anger, hurt, and especially humiliation seeped out of my pores. The first sensible decision I made was to call my sponsor; I needed to expel the vitriol and grieve the loss.

She set me straight, telling me it was God's plan and explaining that I learned of the situation when I was supposed to. It didn't make the pain lessen. She went on, instructing me to go home, pick up the Big Book, and read "Freedom from Bondage."

To sum the story up, the author, an alcoholic, discussed resentments with a clergyman, who said, "If you have a resentment and want to be free of it, you pray for that person; you'll be free of it. If you ask in prayer that whatever you want for yourself be given to them, you will be free of it." So I got down on my knees and prayed, "Dear God, I don't mean this, but please give him *and her* the same blessings you've given me."

I did this every day and night for two weeks straight, and they were right; the resentment began to lift. Working through the pain, I read AA's steps, stories, and related material; the insights they provided were invaluable. Moving toward the light, I clung to a meditation from Melody Beattie's *The Language of Letting Go.* The reflection said, "Seeking revenge will block and hold you back. All you need to do is walk away, stop playing the game, and unhook."

It all sounded simple to do, but as always, it wasn't easy. Grateful for being taught a valuable lesson, I did my best to put it behind me, with the lesson intact. Acceptance helped, as did the decision to open my heart and forgive; for it is forgiveness that releases us and sets us free to walk a separate path. It took me several years to do this, but I did.

Forgiveness heals.

~~~~~~~~

Coming into AA, I was told, "There's only one thing you need to change about your life, and that one thing is everything." They were right, and because I followed GOD (Good Orderly Direction), I found everything began to change because I was changing. The promises written in the Big Book of Alcoholics Anonymous were materializing.

Within the first painstaking year of my recovery, I knew a new freedom and a new happiness. Feelings and emotions, whether painful or not, were felt, processed, and then let go. Finally, I could accomplish what my father suggested years ago, when he encouraged me to let troubles roll off me like water off a duck's back.

The memory of living in chaos, so familiar to me, began to fade away, as I comprehended the word *serenity* and knew peace for the first time. I didn't regret the past nor wish to shut the door on it because every decision I made, good, bad, or indifferent, made me the person I was. But it was vital that I remember those choices.

Another of the promises of AA manifested when the fear of economic insecurity left me. It was a critical issue for me; I rebounded into a marriage because I lacked faith in my ability to provide for myself. Living in the Prostitute's shadow and unable to control it, I sold myself for physical survival by entering a relationship that, for me, was not healthy. Now clear-headed, without the effects of alcohol, I knew I could provide for my well-being, letting go of that fear. I suddenly realized that God was doing for me what I could not do for myself.

Amazing things were going to happen as a result.

~~~~~~~~

The promises of AA were instrumental in my recovery over the next several years, as my parents battled cancer. My mother was first diagnosed in the fall of 2002 with small-cell lung cancer (SCLC), with a five-year survival rate of only 15 percent. She had only quit smoking a couple of years prior to her diagnosis. It was a bombshell to me, as well as to my parents.

However, the gift I was given from the program of recovery was that I learned to be present for my mother. I didn't worry about what would happen if she became incapacitated or died. I took one day at a time with her and cherished all of it. What happened with her cancer was short of a miracle.

The oncologist noticed after her first round of chemotherapy that she was a responder, meaning that the drugs administered to her were killing the cancer cells. The goal of limited-stage SCLC is to cure, which is achieved in 20 to 25 percent of patients. Knowing that I was one of the 10 percent of alcoholics who recover (according to the American Society of Addiction Medicine), I told Mommy she had a better chance than I did.

After her chemotherapy regimen, the doctor had told Mommy she was cured from the SCLC, which was great news. The unwelcome fact was that the vast majority of patients with this type of cancer had it metastasize to the brain. My mother had two options: irradiate her healthy brain to increase her odds for survival or take a chance she was in the 5 percent of those where it didn't spread to the brain. If she chose the latter and lost, she would most likely die.

She opted for radiation and finished her treatment in June 2003. It was just in time for her to enjoy the fiftieth wedding anniversary party I held for my parents on August 22. The moment was a joyous occasion that came between life-altering events for my parents. Less than a year after my mother's diagnosis of SCLC, my father was diagnosed with the exact same cancer.

His reaction was vastly different than my mother's, in that she fought the disease head-on, whereas he was complacent. Perhaps it was his overall health condition; he lived with heart disease, thyroid issues, and emphysema and took a host of medications to treat them. My mother, now feeling better from the chemo and radiation treatments, returned to her role as caretaker.

You could see the decline in my father much more so than my mother. By this time, he was on oxygen but still had enough spunk, wanting to go to Atlantic City for an overnight trip. I accompanied him twice, the last occurring around his birthday, June 9, 2004. During these Daddy dates, we held close, meaningful conversations, which I shall always keep close to my heart.

Just one month later, on July 9, a hospice nurse called, telling me to come home from my day at the beach, to say good-bye to my father. I was in shock; he was just in Atlantic City on Monday and Tuesday.

When I arrived at their house, several family members were saying their farewells to my dad, who laid comatose on a gurney. Within minutes after they left, my dad took his last breath.

I said, "Mommy, Daddy's gone."

She came over to his side and said, "No, he's not; he's still warm."

I had to tell her gently that was because he just passed a few seconds ago.

My mother had been up for almost forty-eight hours, caring for him. Hysterically, I called my cousin to come back to the house, as well as Pat, one of my mother's close coworkers. After notifying the hospice nurse and funeral home, we called the doctor to prescribe a sedative for my mother.

After my father was pronounced and taken away, I went with my cousin to pick up the prescription. Within minutes after taking the pill, my mother fell into a state of drowsiness so deep, we had to carry her upstairs to bed. Carefully removing her skirt and blouse, we tucked her into bed; she went out like a light. We were grateful she was getting the rest she needed.

The next day was Saturday and when I walked into my AA home group meeting, several members noticed something was wrong and quickly came over to me. The emotional support I received was overwhelming; knowing I had a soft place to land with them gave me a solid sense of security.

My dad's viewing was Monday, two days later. Unfortunately, torrential downpours and major flooding prevented many people from attending, but the next day, when his funeral took place, was sunny, without clouds or humidity. All I can remember is being depressed and feeling weighted down, like inside a dark cloud. There was no light for me that day.

A month earlier, I had scheduled a candle party to be held on the Friday night after my father died. I went home the day after his service to prepare the necessary items: the display, folders, and door prizes. My grief was so overwhelming I was unable to perform the tasks, so I turned around and went back to my parents' home to be with my mother.

By the day of the show, I felt the emotional distress lifting, and once more, I drove the twenty miles back to my residence. I was able to finish the task of organizing my kit. The party that evening was successful; sales were over $900, and I earned more than $300 in profit.

Amazed by the short length of time it took me to snap out of my sorrow, I knew it was partly attributed to what I learned in AA. Concerning emotions, I was taught to feel the feelings, process them, and then let them go, which is exactly what I did. I was in awe of being aware of this experience as it unfolded before me.

Debbie Gill

It was all a new way of living for me: to live in the present.

CHAPTER 18

Leaps of Faith, Manifestations, and Miracles

By leaving your comfort zone behind and taking a leap of faith into something new, you find out who you are truly capable of becoming.
~ Unknown ~

Although I had changed dramatically over the past five years, both my professional and personal life remained stuck at a crossroads. I had been a leader for ten years, achieved success in sales, and won incentive trips, but I was ineffective in leadership development, the principal objective of the company, having promoted only one other person to the same rank as myself, unit leader.

In 2005, Jack Canfield spoke at our national annual conference, promoting his new book, *The Success Principles*. I admired his work, and my attention was hooked after hearing him speak. I was motivated to purchase the book immediately after returning home.

Jack wrote about many principles that resonated with my core values. One of them was to always ask for what you want. If you don't ask, the answer is always no. It never occurred to me, as Jack says, that I wouldn't be in a worse position for doing so, but I had everything to gain. That principle, from his chapter "Ask, Ask, Ask," has since remained with me.

Another concept that influenced change within me was a call to action. Jack writes, "There's an enduring axiom of success that says, 'The universe rewards action.'" When you move in the direction of your goals, you will attract things to help you achieve them, including people. It reminded me a guidepost from AA I followed, "If you want what we have, you must do what we do." And what I had to do was get moving.

The more I read, the more I began to lay the groundwork that would transform my life. Being stuck in the ubiquitous daily grind, and meeting the bare minimum, was no longer appealing to me. The pivotal point and segue for me to change was when I learned there was a coaching program based on Jack's success principles.

I hesitated to make the phone call to apply for the program; it was a step outside my comfort zone, mainly because of the six-month commitment attached. After a ninety-minute interview, the evaluator accepted me into the program; it was music to my ears, until I heard the price: $3,500. I didn't know how I was going to pay for it because my divorce had buried me into a hole for $50,000. And despite paying diligently for six years, I still owed over half of it.

Looking at the facts ($26,000 in debt, zero savings, and one credit card with the maximum of $4,000 in available credit), the decision to pay $3,500 was a risky one. My hesitancy was overtaken by an intuitive nudge, a response I never consciously felt before, and it gave me faith. I had faith that when I held myself accountable and took the necessary action, other events would be set into motion.

Saying yes to the program, I took that first leap of intuitive trust by going to the bank and taking out a cash advance. It was critical for me at this point to let go of any fears, trusting the divine would watch over me, if I did the legwork. Following AA's basic advice, to let go and let God, was difficult, but it catapulted me into a life where I began to see manifestations and miracles happen.

The material arrived within days, and I scheduled my coaching sessions. While the outline was strict and demanding, I resolved to dig my heels in and begin. The work was divided into a detailed schedule, and for the first couple of months, it took some time for me to get adjusted. Even though I felt accomplished, an aura of incompleteness shrouded me; I still struggled financially, and my debt had increased.

While speaking to my coach one afternoon, I complained that I wasn't reducing my debt, but, in fact, it was growing.

He said, "Debbie, by saying that, you are attracting more debt, because what you think about, you bring about."

Since my thoughts focused on debt, even though I was working to eliminate it, I attracted more of it.

Hmmm.

It was an enormous wake-up call for me, and my Canfield coach suggested I write the following affirmation on an index card: "Money flows freely and abundantly to me." He suggested that I always carry it with me, so following his advice, I tucked the card away in my pocket with the unflappable belief that it was true.

Miracles do happen. They happen all the time, but many of us don't see them because we aren't open to them. I was ready to open up and experience them; the time had come. A mere eight days passed from the day I wrote those words until they manifested into physical form.

The law of attraction, where "what you think about, you bring about," or simply put, the ability to attract into our lives whatever we are focusing on, became evident to me on a Sunday in late July, when I chauffeured my mother to Atlantic City. Even though I didn't gamble, I enjoyed taking her for a day of playing the slots, plus she gave me a hundred dollars as a thank-you bonus. The casino she chose was the Trump Marina, but after glancing at the various brochures on her kitchen table, I noticed the Borgata offered a twenty-dollar voucher and suggested we go there instead.

That last-minute decision was the catalyst for my miracle.

After we arrived, the thought of saving the hundred dollars crossed my mind; it was the end of July, business was slow, and with travel and national conference expenses to St. Louis next week, things were looking bleak. Only the anticipation of hearing a deeper version of Jack's *Success Principles* in three days, that coming Wednesday, energized my attitude.

The money would come in handy, I thought. But as soon as I glanced over at my mother, that idea quickly evaporated; she gave me the money to enjoy myself, so I started to play. The morning came and went without much luck, but I won enough to be entertained.

At noon, we decided to use our complimentary buffet coupons. We filled our plates, sat down at a nearby table, and began to enjoy our meal. It reminded me of the occasions when my father brought me here on those Daddy dates. Inside, I smiled, savoring those special moments.

It was a little after one o'clock when I tracked down my favorite slot machine, Rich Girl. This particular one-armed bandit, located at the end of a row, was close to the box office ticket sales. I slid my player's card into it, sat down, and sighed, wishing for better luck in the afternoon.

After saying a few words to my dad, like "Do your magic" or "Pick me, pick me," I slid a ten-dollar bill into the machine and began to play. It wasn't more than fifteen minutes later when a siren blared, signaling that someone won the Super Prize Jackpot. Thinking I was just awarded twenty-five dollars in credits because my card was active, I clapped my hands together.

Something was different this time; I caught a split-second flash on my screen saying, "Congratulations!" That was strange; I never saw my screen flash like that before. As I was trying to make sense of the anomaly, my attention focused on the box office's four giant green billboards. I was in disbelief; they flashed white letters that read: "CONGRATULATIONS, Deborah Gill! You just won $35,574!"

My mother and me with the life-size check at the Borgata

My heart stopped, and I was breathless as the reality of what I just read sank in. Adrenaline then took over; I yanked my card out so hard the chain broke and screamed, "That's me! That's me! That's me!" while jumping up and down in circles. My cheeks were flush with excitement.

Security guards, gaming officials, and other Borgata employees rushed over to me saying, "You sure made it easy for us to find you." A waiter offered a tray filled with champagne and chocolate petit fours. I politely passed on the champagne, taking a chocolate, and asked for a bottle of water instead, and most importantly, for them to find my mother.

They quickly located my mom, and in a childlike manner, she asked, "How much did you win? Five thousand dollars?"

"Oh no, Mommy," I told her, "It's a little bit more than that. I won over thirty-five thousand dollars."

Her cheeks plumped as she smiled at my luck.

I kept asking, "Why me? Why me?" and a female security guard looked at me, saying, "Why not you?"

Indeed, why not me?

After a few minutes, the staff presented me with a life-size check and proceeded to parade me and my mother throughout the casino. I waved, feeling like Miss America, and people stopped gambling to applaud, as they congratulated me on my windfall.

It was so surreal. I had to pinch myself to make sure I wasn't dreaming. When they asked how I would prefer my payout, it finally hit me that this was real. After electing to take five hundred dollars in cash and the remainder in a check, I was ready to leave; giving back any of my jackpot was not an option.

Containing my emotions is a trait I had not yet mastered. And winning the Super Prize Jackpot at the Borgata so soon after carrying the affirmation, "Money flows freely and abundantly to me," certainly caused them to unleash in a flurry. The experience not only left me thrilled, it also convinced me to believe in conscious manifestation.

A new concept, one with lasting and invaluable effects, was being downloaded into my consciousness. It convinced me that I was in alignment with the universe; the two aphorisms, "What you think about, you bring about" and "Thoughts become things; choose wise ones," were the source of my ability to attract the things I desired into my life.

My first attempt to test this theory was to have Jack Canfield autograph my copy of *The Success Principles* at national conference. My intention was simple enough, and even with more than eight thousand consultants in attendance, I was confident he would sign my book.

As if the universe heard me, my assigned seat was twelve rows from his promotional table, ensuring with little doubt it would happen. Feeling energized, I made my way toward his table and stepped in line. When it was my turn to get his autograph, I told him my success story and showed him the photo of me holding the large check.

Grinning from ear to ear, I told Jack his coaching program paid off at a rate of 10 to 1: my $3,500 investment went on to realize a gain of over $35,000. He was delighted to hear of my good fortune, as he noted in my book, "To Debbie, my $35,574 winner! Way to go! Love, Jack."

It was exciting to meet Jack, whose work had a positive impact on my life. The next intention on my list, after our photo together, was to have an eight-by-ten copy of it signed. I was certain how this would occur: at our next leadership training seminar, which Jack was hired to lead. My objective was to achieve the promotion and have him sign it there. But that didn't happen.

Telling the universe when and how I wanted things to happen was a big mistake, one I should have recognized as being attached to controlling the outcome. The law of attraction doesn't work that way. I learned that when you let go of the when and how, the universe will manifest your intentions in the way it sees fit. It will happen, when you are laser clear, since laws establish truth.

Simply put, I didn't earn the promotion to attend Jack's workshop because of a limiting belief and untruth I held: "I can't influence people toward leadership." It was a psychic weight that anchored me down and kept me from achieving success.

~~~~~~~~

In January 2007, after a workout at the gym, I went to my office, backpack still slung over my right shoulder. When I sat at my desk, I heard a click, signifying a new email. When I opened the message, it read, "Jack Canfield to Appear on *The Montel Williams Show*." My spirit soared. In order to receive a pair of tickets for next month's taping, I needed to reply to the email, and I promptly did just that.

Anxiously awaiting an answer, I received an unexpected call from the producers of the show, inviting me to preview *The Secret*, the sensationalized movie about the law of attraction, after which they would interview me on my thoughts of how it works.

Unfortunately, I had already seen the movie, and I told them so. The producer thanked me for my time and said they would send me two tickets for the show. My insides were doing somersaults and backflips simultaneously. "I'm getting my picture signed," I sang over and over, swaying my hips and hands in opposite directions, doing the Cabbage Patch dance.

I invited a colleague of mine to the show, and we decided to ride Amtrak to New York City. We arrived ahead of time and enjoyed the various sights and sounds of the city, as we strolled to the studio. By the time we reached our destination, two women were already waiting in line, and we shared our excitement with them.

During the two-hour wait outside, people came from all directions, giving the queue an impression of orderly chaos. Suddenly, the doors flew open, and the staff began collecting our tickets, replacing them with a numbered card, before ushering us into a waiting room.

I was drawn to a woman named Betsy, whose friend was discussing Jack's rags-to-riches tale. We exchanged pleasantries, and I mentioned my recent monetary manifestation when we were interrupted; they were seating the audience.

My feathers began to ruffle as the front seats filled up with individuals who had been waiting behind us. About to elbow my friend and complain, I heard a gravelly voice say, "You ... and you; over there." He pointed in the direction of the front-row seats on stage, and any resentment I had dissipated.

Sitting there, we both showed shock and disbelief on our faces; we needed to contain our excitement. Everything was unfolding perfectly, I thought, as I reached in my bag for the photograph, giving it a gentle pat.

The taping took over four hours, exhausting any hope I had for Jack to sign my picture. In fact, there wasn't even enough time for him to have lunch with Montel; his plane was scheduled to leave within the hour. Although my spirits were dampened, they were overshadowed by a bevy of gifts contributed from the guests, including Montel.

When the show was over and it was time to leave, we filed out in orderly rows. In synchronistic form, Betsy, the woman I met earlier in the day, and I intersected, as we merged. She commented that I manifested great seats. Pushing my lower lip out in a pout, I said, "Yes, I did, but I didn't get my picture signed."

At this, Betsy chimed in, "Well, I know his training director. If you trust me, I can have it signed for you."

Immediately, I heard the music from the old television show *The Twilight Zone* go off in my head. *Of course you can have my photo*, I thought, handing her the eight-by-ten glossy. I had the negative.

Witnessing synchronicity unfold finally embedded a truth within me: Let go of the how in the way things happen. My picture wasn't signed the way I set it up to be signed, but it was signed. Three weeks later, I received the photograph back with the inscription: "To my $35,000 winner! Jack Canfield."

My signed eight-by-ten glossy with Jack Canfield

~~~~~~~~~

The more I let go of how I wanted things to happen and trusted the signs the universe gave to me, the more synchronistic events took place in my life. It was the beginning of the magical part of the energetic world that continues to unfold and expand in the wonderment of my life.

Being born an extrovert has had its challenges, and the one that is always waiting is the inability to manage my enthusiasm. There appeared to be a channel, however, that would allow my animation to come alive, without me having to spout off. The avenue appeared when I noticed a question posed in the Saturday Lifestyle section of my local newspaper.

Gary Soulsman, the spiritual writer for Gannett's *The News Journal,* was compiling various viewpoints on the commercially successful movie The Secret: whether you believed in it or thought it all a big hoax. You were invited to email your experience directly to him. Feeling lighthearted for a moment, I placed the paper aside, vowing to come back to it. I was facing another, more critical situation: my dog, Frankie, was paralyzed and just had surgery that morning.

The following morning, I emailed Gary, summarizing the events over the past six months. He called the next evening and asked me several questions regarding my beliefs about how the law of attraction worked. After a brief conversation, he told me that my story was remarkable and he would like to interview me. He also added that a photographer would join him, for snapping a picture of me with my vision board and life-size check.

I readily agreed and set the meeting for that Thursday at one o'clock. Gary and the photographer arrived promptly, and he proceeded with his questions, such as, "How has the law of attraction operated in your life" and "What materialized from your thoughts?" After ninety minutes and several photo shots, the interview was over.

As they were leaving, Gary said the article would be ready for press in three weeks and to look for it around that time. The interim felt like the commercial for Heinz, the slow-moving ketchup: anticipation. It was a long three weeks, but the wait was worth it.

Photo from The News Journal

As soon as the paper came, I tore it open, rifling through the pages the same way I used to when I was five, until I found the Lifestyle section, and there I was, front and center. A sense pride began to rise inside of me, but there was also disbelief. Could this be happening to me? It felt like I was in a trance.

The article began with the story of me winning the Super Prize Jackpot but delved deeper into the changes I initiated in my life. Gary interviewed other spiritualists who were quoted, but my account was both the opening and closing segments of the article. The intention to share these synchronistic experiences and the manifesting of my intentions was validated.

Two weeks later, my joy took a nosedive. Sadly, I awoke one morning to find Frankie in extreme distress, gasping for air. I knew the situation was dire, and my fear grew as I fumbled to dial the vet from Penn, while cradling my dog. As I was speaking with the doctor, Frankie took his last breath and died in my arms.

My world collapsed, as I sobbed uncontrollably, screaming, "Frankie, don't die; please, Frankie, please don't go." I was in a state of hysteria, hyperventilating, and trying to think of what to do next. Still holding onto Frankie, I called a friend, and explained through my tears what happened. She arrived within minutes, calmed me down, and drove us to the vet's office.

Frankie's death devastated me, and my grief was unrelenting; it increased by the day. Even after several months, my anguish prevented me from processing his death and moving forward. The feeling was baffling, having worked through my father's death by following an approach I learned from AA on healing: "Feel your feelings, process them, let them go."

Soon afterward, I made the connection for the delay in healing from Frankie's death; it was the catalyst for the spiritual connection I would have with my dad. That bond came about one day as I was walking my other dog, Chessie.

Wanting to be rid of my grief, I looked up to the blue sky and cried, "Daddy, I need to know Frankie is in your arms, just like the picture I gave you for Father's Day, and I need to know now. I need to find a penny right now." Asking for a penny was an arbitrary choice, but one I knew from the adage "pennies from heaven."

The words were barely out of my mouth when, five steps later, I saw a penny on the ground. Stunned, I called Father Bill after I picked the coin up, sharing my experience, and was on the phone with him when I found another one. I quickly snatched the second one off the ground, held it up to heaven, and told my dad he was a comedian. He always was a tease, and I'm confident this was his cue that he heard me.

Throughout my sorrow, I made every effort to be patient with myself. Reading spiritual and personal growth books helped, so I dusted off one of my favorites, *The Four Agreements*, by Don Miguel Ruiz. The Toltec wisdom he writes about nourished my soul and aided my sobriety; I envisioned a similar outcome for this unhappy time. I was not disappointed by this insight written in the book:

"If you live in the present moment, you have no time to miss anyone or anything."

~~~~~~~~

The next few months were challenging; it had been a couple of years since my mother underwent prophylactic cranial irradiation, and the long-term side effects on her brain were becoming much more obvious, even dangerous. Several times, while driving thirty minutes to have her hair done, she got lost and had to call the stylist to come get her. Discovering that she had difficulty following directions troubled me greatly, and I started to consider what should be done about it.

The other prominent change in my mother was her ability to communicate effectively. She confused words, making it extremely difficult to comprehend what she was trying to say, as well as what she wrote. It didn't make sense. Her struggle to remember words not only aggravated herself, it also tested my patience. I finally decided it was easier to nod my head yes and agree with whatever she said.

The breaking point came when I followed my mother for her monthly checkup with the oncologist. After I casually mentioned to him that she got lost a couple of times while driving, he immediately said he was revoking her license. She would not be allowed to drive anymore. My guilt was overwhelming as my mother pleaded with him not to take away her driving privileges. The last time she got behind the wheel of a car was to go home that day, and it was my all fault.

For the next few weeks, I drove up to my mother's house every other day, chauffeuring her from one appointment to another. Many of them were located near where I lived, so an extra two-and-a-half to three hours each day was spent on the highway, time I didn't have to spare. I needed to come up with a solution, fast.

Knowing it would take a miracle for my mother to move, I began to drop little hints about hiring her as my secretary; I needed someone to wrap door prizes for my shows, send out invitations, and do other simple but time-consuming tasks. Somehow, I needed to convey the message that I needed her; she was needed.

I knew I had her hooked when I told her I was thinking about building an addition to the house.

She asked, "How big?" and I replied, "Big."

That was all it took. Taking action, I promptly called a subcontractor and began to draw up floor plans for a living area that would fit her furniture, as well as a master bedroom, bath, walk-in closet, and private entrance. There would be a sliding glass door adjoining the dining room for her to come and go into the main house.

The project was completed in just over two months, and she was moved by the first week of January. I was now the full-time caretaker for my mother, the most challenging yet rewarding job I ever held. Knowing I was about to put my life on hold for an indefinite amount of time, I asked God for guidance and grace. I would need both for the next two years.

CHAPTER 19

Letting Go of Limiting Beliefs

If you accept a limiting belief, then it will become a truth for you.
~ Louise Hay ~

Living in the present moment is necessary for creating the life you desire, and even though I was endeavoring to do so, I found myself frequently wandering into the future, as well as the past. When in the future, I told myself stories, creating fantasies that didn't exist. When in the past, I reinforced my lack of success with limiting beliefs.

In the constant pursuit for enlightenment to learn more about myself, the Seeker archetype continued to thrive. During the first weekend of March 2009, I attended a spiritual retreat, an action-packed event that completely revamped the course of my life and threw me into overdrive. On the agenda: a board-breaking exercise, a practice where you shatter a one-inch-thick board with your bare hands. James instructed us to write a limiting belief on one side of the board and write what was the truth on the other.

My limiting belief was, "I can't influence people toward leadership." In my mind, this was a truth for me; in my fourteen-year career, I had influenced only one consultant to become a leader. In plain English: I sucked. On the flip side, the real truth I wrote was, "I can influence people toward leadership."

Seeing that an action is possible is instrumental in enabling you to believe you can do it too. To illustrate how you successfully break a board, shattering whatever is holding you back, the speaker called for a volunteer. A young woman stepped onto the stage and watched as he demonstrated the procedure. He then held a board for her to break, and after six attempts, she broke the board. The audience stood on their feet and cheered.

The underlying suggestion was that if she could break it, then everyone else could also. And we were about to find out, as all the participants lined up with their boards. The sounds of wood snapping could be heard echoing throughout the hall.

During the short wait until it was my turn, I could feel my heart begin to race, as the adrenalin pumped, creating a bead of sweat on my forehead and making my mouth dry. Moving toward my designated spot, I took a deep breath, pushed aside any fear, and whacked the board, using the heel of my hand. As I fell forward, I heard it snap, confirming the break.

A sense of self-worth, an attitude I was unaccustomed to, began to develop, and it grew when I was assigned a new mentor later in the week. With her guidance, and the chains of my limiting belief broken, synchronistic events appeared so rapidly during the next six months; it cemented a knowing, anchoring it deep within me.

My new advisor, Teresa, outlined a plan of action that I was to follow the next month, which included organizing a sizable guest event, a new skill for me to hone. The affair was designed to be a hostess appreciation celebration, with the intention of sponsoring them into the business and ultimately developing them into leaders. Teresa was traveling to Delaware from the Midwest to assist with the details. Working with her established a new resolve within me, so I rolled up my sleeves and got to work.

Life began to swirl, and positive responses to my offers to join the business or climb the ladder increased in speed with each passing day, and within six weeks, I influenced two women into leadership positions. By eliminating the negativity from my thoughts, more people were drawn to me, and I successfully sponsored eight people, a record high for me.

I was developing a new awareness; there was a correlation between my thoughts and beliefs and what materialized in my life. Just as energy comes before matter, thought comes before form, and so it became evident that my thoughts became things.

As spring turned into summer, my experience and connection with conscious manifesting began to increase exponentially. A Facebook friend from Atlanta, who registered for the conference as a new consultant, decided to step into a leadership position. Where was conference? Why, Atlanta, of course. She became a leader on August 1.

I was in the zone, inspired by the numerous meaningful coincidences that appeared in my life. By the end of August, in a five-month period, I influenced five women to become leaders, and by doing so, I advanced to the rank of regional leader on September 1, 2009. It seemed remarkable to me, as I compared the two results: one leader in fourteen years versus five leaders in five months.

Anything is possible, but yet again, in the blink of an eye, it can all be gone again.

~~~~~~~~

Less than three months later, my mother came home from a day of Christmas shopping and dinner, not feeling well. Her once-a-week caretaker, Donna, who I hired shortly after Mommy moved in to give me a little break, had taken her out. Donna said

Mommy didn't eat much and her back was hurting, so I gave her one of my 800 milligram ibuprofen and put her to bed. I wasn't prepared for what was about to happen.

The next day was my first regional meeting as a regional leader. I had prepared for weeks, delegating sections to my five new leaders, and had the entire 2010 product line in boxes, ready to set up. Something other than nerves woke me up in the middle of the night, and when I went downstairs, Mommy was in the kitchen. When I asked her what she was doing up, she said she didn't know. I told her to go back to bed.

At seven o'clock in the morning, I got out of bed and noticed my mother wasn't in the kitchen like she usually was. As I neared the sliding glass door, I saw her slumped over, holding a bag of dog treats, with Chessie by her side. Inquiring why she didn't go to bed, she told me she didn't know. I became increasingly anxious when a few minutes later, she came to the kitchen and put two slices of boiled ham in her cereal bowl. She wasn't even aware she didn't have her dentures in.

Mommy went downhill as the morning progressed. I called Teresa, my upline leader, in Michigan for guidance; she advised me to contact my leaders and inform them they were to fill in for me; my mother's health was rapidly declining and I needed to be with her. The despair I felt about my mother's condition far exceeded any disappointment I had about missing my first opportunity to lead the regional meeting. Latrina, her hospice nurse, visited with her, checking her vitals, and told me she was dying.

For the next two days, Mommy remained on her sofa while I occasionally fed her some pudding. Anything she uttered was gibberish and incoherent. I called Father Roger from our parish to come give her the Last Rites. Family came to say their goodbyes. I was numb, in a state of denial, and it felt like time stood still. *This can't be happening*, I thought. *I'm not ready to say goodbye.*

Thanksgiving Day was here. I carried Mommy to her bedroom and got into bed with her, chatting about all the things I remembered we did together as I grew up. "Mommy, I remember when you curled my hair in rollers and then put the dryer cap on my head. Do you remember those old-fashioned dryers with the hose attached? Do you remember making macaroni trees?"

I stayed and talked with her constantly, giving her permission to go and be with Daddy, Donnie, and baby Michael, only taking a break when someone would come for an hour or so to sit with her. She became comatose and wasn't eating, but more importantly she wasn't drinking water. At night, I set the alarm every four hours to give her morphine.

By Sunday, after over four days with no food or water, I told her to please go to the light, that it would be easier for me if she did. Still, she lingered. I can only guess she didn't want to leave me alone, without any family. My heart broke at the sight of her lying on the bed: she had shriveled to a mere eighty pounds, her bones were protruding from her slight frame, and her fingernails and toenails turned a dark shade of purple. It wasn't until Tuesday evening, December 1, that she took her last breath, shattering my world. When she died, a piece of me died with her.

Major depression sank in, preventing me from performing not only the essential tasks to remain a regional leader but also daily, mundane ones. I felt the cords of psychic weight holding me down, tethering me to the earth, and I was unable to shake loose from it for months.

I lost my region. I lost my way in life. I lost my sense of purpose. I was unable to understand why the grief from my mother's death persisted. Bewildered at the inability to process my emotions the same way I did with my father, I spoke with my spiritual director. What she explained to me made perfect sense. She said that the relationship I had with my father was complete, but the one with my mother was not. It took over nine months for me to come to terms with her death, bringing our relationship to fruition, and to bounce back from the heaviness of my heart.

~~~~~~~~

Random circumstances, with fortuitous results, occurred several times during the next few years. A clear consequence of my decision to let go of financial insecurity was that large sums of money seemed to track me like a radar and drop into my lap, without warning. After several failed attempts to locate my parents (who at this time were deceased), American Stock Transfer & Trust Company finally got in touch with me. Much to my surprise, there were undisclosed stocks not included in my parents' financial portfolio. The first settlement was a claim for $1,800 in PNC stock, with a second one six months later, for $25,000 in the same stock.

Another bag of money that fell from the sky came a few months after my mother had passed away. A relative called to inform me that Mommy had been a beneficiary of her mother-in-law's estate and was entitled to $25,000. The inheritance would now go to me instead, because my mother was deceased.

One additional out-of-the-blue windfall came after I found an ad in the newspaper for an unclaimed account at ING (now Capital One 360) in my dad's name. When I called the bank, the representative told me they weren't at liberty to disclose the amount, but it was at least twenty-five dollars. After faxing the necessary paperwork, I received a check three days later for $10,288.

Just as recently as October 2016, there were unclaimed funds from the state of Delaware in my father and brother's names. While this amount was much less than the previous ones,

$433 was still a bonus, and, like all the others, one I wasn't expecting.

Why was this happening?

The further I opened myself up, the more I became aware of shifts in my perception. Miracles were happening monthly, weekly, and sometimes daily. Life, for me, became more like a river flowing downstream than that of a salmon struggling to go against the current. The art of allowing, letting go and living in present time, became instrumental in my healing and manifesting.

Accept what is, let go of what was,
have faith in what will be.

CHAPTER 20

The Healing Path of the Wounded Healer

*Only the wounded healers, and only they can heal to the extent
they have healed themselves.*
~ Carl Jung ~

Reflecting on the past fifty-plus years that I've lived this incredibly blessed yet often painful life, I am filled with awe and gratitude. The path I traveled has been full of twists, turns, thorns, and black holes, but with the grace of God, I have found the answer I was searching for so desperately: truth. Now, it's just a matter of living one day at a time, finding a way to recover each time lightning strikes.

~~~~~~~~~

One day, as I was reviewing *The Power of Archetypes* video from a workshop Caroline Myss held, I heard her words in a different light. Myss clarified, "Tenth Chakra [Mystical] Law states [when talking to the divine]: God, if I am to do the work of this archetype [in my case, the Wounded Healer], I trust, and have faith, that you'll take care of all the coincidences and synchronicities for that to happen."

As I sat at my computer listening, her words bowled me over; their meaning began to formulate in my mind. I've experienced many serendipitous events, as well as some synchronistic ones, walking down this path; the series of sudden windfalls now made sense. At this stage of my life, I found it wasn't possible to work full-time *and* study Caroline Myss's teachings to the extent where I could convey them in a proficient manner. That money out of the blue was used to pay off my mortgage, allowing me to reduce my work hours, cutting them in half, leaving ample time for my education. My trust in God, in a way, allowed my mortgage to be paid.

~~~~~~~~

My introduction to Caroline Myss came at a time when I was searching for alternative ways to deal with the unexplained side effects of the lightning strike I incurred in 1978. They emerged once more, only now manifesting as extreme nerve pain in my lower back and leg. After several years of pain management that included injections, invasive tests, and increased dosages of medications, mostly narcotics, I made the decision to seek alternative, holistic healing.

In May 2010, a friend suggested I explore Ayurveda, a five-thousand-year-old science of life from India. Its central tenet is designed to bring the body back into balance, enabling it to heal itself. Following his advice, I googled it and found a professional who operated a practice nearby. I made an appointment and began to follow the discipline, with her assistance. After a few weeks, she introduced me to the owner of the yoga studio where she had an office.

Although Ayurveda and yoga are separate and distinct, they do complement each other, and he suggested I try a nonheated class to help with alignment and movement principles. Signing up the first week in June, I came to class twice a week for four weeks. Next, I enrolled in a beginners' course, where I had access to unlimited sessions for a month, and then I registered for unlimited classes.

It was sometime later in the fall when I became aware of Caroline Myss's book, *Why People Don't Heal and How They Can*. Shortly thereafter, I learned she was speaking on the Hay House "I Can Do It" Caribbean Cruise in February 2011, so I signed up for the eight-day event at sea.

The cruise's itinerary included a panel of eight well-known authors and speakers in the spiritual and personal-development industry. Each speaker held a two-hour workshop at a designated date and time, leaving enough space in between for downtime and shore excursions. It had everything I was searching for to strengthen my health, both emotionally and physically.

During my time on the cruise, I noticed coincidences were happening more frequently than ever. After Caroline's seminar on her new book, *Defy Gravity*, the next scheduled workshop was Sonia Coquette's. She was very experiential, and we often got up to dance. For one of the exercises, a partner was required, so John, the man sitting next to me, became mine. When he mentioned he only came to support his wife and didn't believe all this foo-foo stuff, I suggested that he keep an open mind.

The next workshop featured John Holland, a well-known psychic and medium. When he started to receive messages, he directed his attention to an audience member seated in the balcony, who was also named John. When asked if he recently landscaped his yard, John answered yes.

Well," John said, "Your mother-in-law [the spirit coming through] doesn't approve of it."

His wife, who was sitting next to him, spoke up and said she didn't know why, but she tore the whole thing apart and completely revamped the design of the garden. After the wife provided this information, John added, "By the way, she approves of the new layout."

The session ended just before lunch, so I took the elevator to the dining area. During the ride up, it made one stop, and John, my partner from Sonia's workshop, stepped in. It was just the two of us, so I asked him if he went to John Holland's event, and if so, had he heard about the man with the landscaping issue. He said, "Yes, I did, and it was me he was talking to! I am a believer now." With the sizable number of people on the ship, what were the odds this would happen?

Synchronicity was playing out before my very eyes. But there's more.

Later in the evening, after the formal dinner with my new friend, Russell, I went to the casino with twenty dollars for some fun. After playing for an hour or so and winning twice the amount I started with, I went to cash out only to find my card got stuck in the machine; it had demagnetized.

I dashed down to the front desk for a replacement room card; I was pressed for time since both my card and money remained in the one-armed bandit. Making my way back to the casino, I was skipping down the hall on Deck 3 when I heard a voice from behind me call out, "Who's the lady with the great legs?" Thinking it was Russell, I turned around, only to be surprised to see Wayne Dyer, the father of motivation and self-help guru; he had just complimented me. Wayne was one of the most well-known authors and speakers in the spiritual growth field, writing *The Erroneous Zones*, a book that sold over thirty-five million copies.

Pausing until he caught up to me, I felt a shiver pass through my spine; I was starstruck. He shook my hand and introduced himself, saying modestly, "I'm Wayne."

I melted and started to babble something about wanting to get my book signed. He said, "There's always tomorrow."

We also spoke about missing our yoga, and I told him it was the anniversary of my being struck by lightning. In all, we spent fifteen minutes conversing; it was a highlight of the cruise for me.

The next day, I spent the morning horseback riding on the beach, as well as in the ocean. During the excursion, I met another woman who, like me, was finding synchronicities at every turn. We walked back to the ship after our ride and spotted Wayne sitting on a beach chair. I approached him, recalling our chance encounter the previous night, and asked permission to have a picture taken with him; he obliged.

Picture of Wayne Dyer and me he signed "Legs"

For the final seminar on the cruise, Cheryl Richardson, a best-selling author, coach, and speaker, had people line up with questions. She co-wrote the book *You Can Create an Exceptional Life* with Louise Hay and has a weekly radio talk show on www.HayHouseRadio.com. Eager to find a reason for my single status, I scurried up front and got the second spot. After asking why she thought I wasn't in a committed relationship, I added, "My father told me never to depend on a man."

Cheryl must have heard something relevant because she invited me up to the stage to sit by her. She posed several questions about our relationship, and after a lengthy and personal conversation — in front of seven hundred people — suggested that instead of looking for a man, I look for my feminine energy.

Cheryl even went as far as to ask the male members in the audience, if they saw me, to open a door for me. As a result, not only were plenty of doors held open for me the rest of the day, but I was also served water at lunch and dinner. Two additional coincidences or synchronicities occurred. One happened when Cheryl gave me a signed copy of her book; it was the only speaker's I didn't purchase. And the other was that evening, when a tarot card was left on my bed: it read, "I balance my masculine and feminine energy."

~~~~~~~~

The following September, I went to New York City with a friend to attend another *I Can Do It* event; this one featured Caroline Myss as well as several other spiritual teachers. It was Myss's ideas and principles on healing that I hungered for; I desperately wanted to heal my body from the knifelike nerve pain and get off the narcotics that were prescribed to me.

For an entire year, I dove into her books, reading one after another, taking a look within to examine the issues that prevented me from healing. The inner work was as brutal and intense as my physical pain; it felt like I was tearing open an old scar with a serrated knife, with the same force you'd gut a fish. As I peeled away layers of painful wounds, I reflected in my journal, continuing to pray, and did my best to stay in present time.

At the same time I was striving to bring my emotional issues to the surface, the doctors kept prescribing higher doses of painkillers; my daily intake increased to three morphine tablets and four oxycodones. Functioning under that level of medication was problematic, but the thought of unbearable withdrawal symptoms held me in the shadow of both the Addict and the Saboteur, reconsidering my desire to heal.

An unusual phenomenon occurred, however, when I awoke one day in February 2012. I made the decision to heal my body, freeing myself not only from pain but the harmful drugs. Within two weeks, I found I was no longer in pain and had no signs of withdrawal. I was incredibly grateful but also very confused. I had no idea how that happened. People just don't wake up and say, "I'm healing today," and heal.

I continued to excavate.

~~~~~~~~

The following September, when I heard Caroline speak again, her words resonated with me; was it her knowledge on a subject that attracted me, the way she delivered it, or both? The archetypes in me—Addict, Student, and Seeker—all clamored for more information. However, I wasn't able to connect the dots or put my finger on precisely what they wanted.

Myss touched on several topics in her book, *Sacred Contracts*, including archetypes, and I was captivated. She went on to explain their functions, describing how the four Survival ones provide you with opportunities during your lifetime to develop self-esteem, as you are not born with it. It was fascinating. It felt like I was physically being pulled toward her, like a magnet, and told her so as she signed my book.

Immediately after arriving home, I pulled *Sacred Contracts* off my bookshelf. Leafing through the tabbed and highlighted sections, it dawned on me I had only read up to the chapter "Speaking Archetypes." Taking a second look made clear the reason for why I stopped: I had no idea what they were or what they did.

Several days passed, and as I continued to write this story, a thought suddenly came to mind; I needed to be a student of hers to learn about these things called archetypes. I casually mentioned this to my friend, a fellow yoga teacher. The next day, I received a catalog from Kripalu, an organization I didn't recognize.

Thumbing through the magazine, I realized it was for an Ayurveda and yoga institute and was drawn to take a closer look. Casually flipping a page, my heart stopped at the photo at the bottom left; it was a picture of Caroline Myss, who was holding a weekend workshop on the power of archetypes. Amazed at having said one day that I needed to be a student of hers, and the next day having my request granted, I felt goose bumps run up and down my arms. When signs show up, and your intuition gives you a nudge, you are wise to listen, so I immediately registered for the seminar.

At the end of "The Power of Archetypes" workshop, another force, resembling an energetic light, pulled me to redirect the course of my life, as it permeated my physical body. A deep inspiring conviction remained, which motivated me to pursue the wisdom and teachings of Caroline Myss. In spite of being unaware of where this path would lead, I knew it was necessary to quit my leadership position, trusting the process as it unfolded before me.

Not only did I find myself veering off the highway of what was expected of me in my career, the underlying theme of this book took a dramatic turn as well. By following my intuition, I was prompted to expose the wounds of my soul and in the process discerned I was on the healing path of the Wounded Healer.

For me, it was a calling, and I had no choice; it was magnetic and all-consuming. My resolve to help others in their healing was, and is, just as intense as it was in Alcoholics Anonymous, which encourages members to be of service as they reach out to other suffering alcoholics. As Caroline so eloquently states, "A calling is an awakening of your soul's visionary skills and graces so that you become an agent of transformation in the world. The 'how' is never your choice."

It all made sense to me now. Having had a spiritual awakening, I was called to go deeper, discovering and healing my wounds so that I could be an agent of transformation in the world. Familiarity with archetypes, my experience with the program of Alcoholics Anonymous, as well as the discernment of the physical, energetic, and spiritual or mystical realms, along with many of Myss's other teachings, were the conduit for this to happen.

~~~~~~~~

A few months later, in June, I went to a workshop Caroline was conducting at Miraval, a resort in Tucson. During the five-day workshop, called "Archetypes, Who Are You?" she aimed two significant observations directly at me. Although the remarks were painful to hear, their intentions came with love and compassion. I am eternally grateful for her spanking, for without it, I would not be the person I am today.

The first time she gave me a slap on the wrist was during dinner a couple of nights in. Because there were only thirty-one students, Caroline dined with us, migrating from table to table. That evening, she sat to my left, with another person in between. The topic was the Child archetype, and I mentioned I was the Invisible Child. Caroline looked directly at me and said, "Yes, and you have the need to be seen. When is enough, enough?"

Ouch. I felt a punch in the stomach.

During the following day's lecture, I posed a question about being addicted to love. Caroline said I was brave to have the conversation on this topic; she continued, "One form of the Addict is the lover, and because attention is so important to you, the Femme Fatale is an archetype you have. Even if, when, your addiction is manageable, the Femme Fatale is very much a part of your persona."

Furthermore, she explained I would come to know my Femme Fatale in some way because it's part of who I am; it's part of my beauty. I learned that because I put the archetype in the shadow, I treated myself negatively and that I needed to come to terms with getting to know myself outside of a negative way.

Double ouch, but she was spot-on in her reading of my archetypal pattern.

~~~~~~~~~

In the ensuing months and years, my spiritual connection to everything began to blossom. One unforgettable incident occurred the very next month in July, when I opened my front door; there was a tiger swallowtail butterfly sitting on my front step. Without a thought or knowing why, I shouted, "Daddy!" Getting on my knees, I placed my index finger near him, and to my amazement, he climbed on. After two separate occasions of the butterfly staying on my finger, I decided to video this unusual event.

For a third time, I whirled my hand around, with the butterfly cleaving to my finger, as if to show him a 360-degree panorama. Lingering for more than a minute, he flitted off and began to fly back and forth, as though inviting me to play. Aware of the time that passed, I said, "Daddy, I'll be back in a couple of hours. I have to go teach yoga."

Imagine my surprise when I returned from class to see the butterfly still resting in the flowerbed between two garden statues

I saved from my parents' house. As if on cue, the back-and-forth banter of playful fun began once more, and I found myself running around a tree, chasing a butterfly no one else could see.

My father in the form of a tiger swallowtail

After more than four hours of amusement, the butterfly did not want to leave. Having to turn the compost before dark, I said, "Daddy, I'm going to the backyard because I have some work to do." After fifteen or twenty minutes of lifting and flipping wet compost, my back started to ache, and I said to myself, "If you're really my dad, come to the backyard."

My jaw dropped open when I saw the tiger swallowtail fluttering around the sandstone patio. Pinching myself, I thought, what butterfly comes when called? The answer was obvious: the butterfly that inhabits my dad's spirit. The total time I spent with the butterfly — Daddy — was just over five hours. As twilight fell, I walked around the side of the house, with the butterfly in tow. Just as I reached the front yard, it circled the tree three times and flew off into the night.

Two days later, I found his delicate remains. He had died but fortunately was not consumed by a bird, grasshopper, or other predator. While the tiger swallowtail butterfly lives only a month, this one lived long enough to connect with me spiritually, allowing me the privilege of holding it. Several years later, when in Sedona, I found a butterfly glass box of the same species; it was a perfect fit for his final resting place.

Three years later, during the same month, I was gardening in my backyard when I saw a pair of tiger swallowtails flutter by and gracefully land on the grass next to me. Thinking my mother had joined my dad for a reunion, I gently bent over, picking up one and then the other. The experience left me with no doubt my parents were watching over and guiding me in life.

Mommy and Daddy along for the ride

~~~~~~~~

The following year, I planned to go on Caroline's cruise to Fiji, but it was canceled, so I signed up for the "Awaken Your

Spirit" cruise with John Holland and Sonia Choquette. It was true to its name, and I came away increasing my intuitive abilities, experiencing more instances of conscious manifesting and synchronicity.

In one of the sessions, after opening our creative side by dancing and just letting go, we were to select a partner, someone we didn't know. We were going to use a psychic tool called psychometry (which means "measure of the soul"), the practice of holding someone's possession and then reading it.

Since I didn't know the woman sitting next to me, we decided to pair up and practice on each other. She gave me her necklace, and I held it in my hand and closed my eyes. John said if we couldn't read anything, to just make something up, but I didn't have to.

The first thing I felt (clairsentient) was being on a farm; everything was green. I then saw (clairvoyant) the word farm capitalized in white block letters. What followed was the pitter-patter sound (clairaudient) of little feet, so I thought she must have a lot of siblings or children.

When I described my intuitive outcomes, she told me she lived on her grandfather's farm in Iowa, and it was also where he happened to raise puppies for many years. Although my ability to receive this information by tuning in and reading her energy from a piece of jewelry was real, it surprised me.

On the last day, our port of call was Curacao, an island I had been to twice before. Wanting to do a little shopping, I set off alone; when I got into town, I passed a shop with a dress that caught my attention. Deciding to come back later, I went on to explore the island.

After a couple of hours, I was getting tired but wanted to return to the dress shop. It took fifteen minutes to locate, only to find out they sold the dress in my size. Disappointed but undeterred, I picked out several things to try on. Turning around, a woman bumped into me, causing me to lose my grip on the wooden hangers and drop the dresses onto the floor.

A man sitting on a nearby stool said, "*Entschuldigen.*" Knowing it was an apology in German, I countered with, "*Sie bitte. Verstehen sie?*" It meant, "Please, do you understand?" We all laughed as they remarked about my German skills, of which I was surprised came back after twenty years.

They were a delightful couple, and though I had never asked anyone before where in Germany they were from, I asked them. Barbara said they were from Stuttgart, near Heilbronn. Hmm, I thought. Heilbronn was close to Ellhofen (pop. 3,340), Karl's hometown. So I asked her if she knew where Ellhofen was, and she went, "Noooo, we're from Ellhofen, but no one knows where it is. That's why I say Stuttgart or Heilbronn."

It was getting weird now, so I asked her if she heard of the Webers. Again, she went, "Noooo, Franz and Greta? We're their property managers."

"Yes, Franz and Greta," I replied back. "They're my former in-laws."

I almost fell over. What were the chances that a girl from Delaware would bump into business associates of her ex-in-laws who were from a tiny village in Germany, with a population of 3,340, in a small dress shop, on the island of Curacao, in the middle of February?

If that encounter wasn't evidence I had become more open to following my intuition, the experience I had on my way home from the airport was. Driving home, a thought was downloaded into my consciousness: the name of a yoga business, Go Within Yoga. The name was perfect; too perfect, I thought, for the domain, dot com, to be available, but the urge to investigate the possibility created anxiety within me, making it difficult to drive.

As soon as I pulled in the driveway, I ran to my office and searched for the domain. I could not find it, which meant it was open. What happened next continues to amaze me. Unaware I was doing so, I consciously manifested Go Within Yoga through the chakras. It wasn't until two years after my studio was opened that I read Anodea Judith's book, *Creating on Purpose*, and I realized what I had done.

To explain as simply as possible, my original thought, the name for the website, www.gowithinyoga.com (energy), came into existence (matter), after only two months. The following clarification helps break it down into the home of each chakra, beginning with the top.

Go Within Yoga was the idea (chakra seven) I received out of the sea of infinite possibilities, and it was moved down into my stream of consciousness. The seventh chakra, or Crown Chakra, is located at the top of the head; it gives us access to higher states of consciousness as we open to what is beyond our personal preoccupations and visions.

I then began to visualize in my mind's eye (chakra six) what it would look like and when it would happen. The sixth chakra, or third eye, is located on the forehead, between the eyebrows; it is the center of intuition and foresight, and its function is driven by the principle of openness and imagination.

I began telling others (chakra five) about my vision, which provided me feedback and support. The fifth chakra, or throat chakra, is located at the center of the neck at the level of the throat, and it is the passage of the energy between the lower parts of the body and the head. The principle of expression and communication drive its function.

The support I received, in turn, allowed the relationships with others (chakra four) to work with, serve, and supply me with the necessary materials to form. The fourth chakra, or heart chakra, is located in the center of the chest; it colors our life with compassion, love, and beauty. Driven by the principles of transformation and integration, the fourth chakra is said to bridge earthly and spiritual aspirations.

I then moved myself and others toward my goal using my free will (chakra three) and breaking my vision down into specific tasks to accomplish. The third chakra, or solar plexus chakra, is located in the upper part of the belly; it is characterized by the expression of will, personal power, and mental abilities. The energy of the third chakra is mobilized when we assert ourselves in the world.

As I began to see the outcome take place, it ignited my fire (chakra two), and everything I wanted came into existence, from my turquoise furniture to a Buddha wall painting. The second chakra, or sacral chakra, is located three inches below your naval and is associated with the emotional body, sensuality, and creativity. The principle of pleasure directs the function of the sacral chakra.

Each step evolved fluidly, as did my enthusiasm. My aspiration came into existence (chakra one). The first chakra, or root chakra, is located at the base of the spine. The first chakra provides the foundation on which we build our life, and it is where we ground ourselves into the earth, anchoring our energy into the manifest world.

When I completed all these steps, my vision, arising out of a thought, entered into form as my new business, Go Within Yoga. It was up and running two months later.

My journey on the healing path continues.

Epilogue

Life has been a series of highs and lows, twists and turns, and more drama and chaos than a person would wish to have, but one thing I know for sure: I have no regrets and would not choose to do anything differently, not one thing. You may think I'm crazy. I am not.

Every choice I made, and every decision I didn't, brought me to be the person I am today, living in a place of freedom. It wasn't easy, and I often forged ahead begrudgingly, but I always knew that I would heal from my past wounds if I did the work.

It is not only painful but also frightening to look within, to chisel away old beliefs and patterns of behavior, replacing them with new ones that lead to your empowerment. Learning what my archetypes were and how they influenced me was a crucial factor in helping me do that, along with Caroline Myss, whose wisdom has had the greatest influence in my spiritual life.

Without Caroline's guidance, without her setting me straight, without her love and compassion, I would not be the person I am, living the truth of who I am. She taught me how to develop self-esteem, to not treat myself negatively, that nothing in life is personal, and how to be courageous and humble in the face of adversity. Caroline has led by example and is a person I can only hope one day to emulate. There have been many people, spiritual teachers, friends, support groups who have helped me on the path of the Wounded Healer, but Caroline is the one who has given me the most knowledge, support, and encouragement.

Caroline and me in 2016

My journey from the shadow to the light has not ended, nor will it ever. I realize I am who I am, and I do the best with what God gave me; sometimes, I do it better than other times. Learning to let go and let God was a lesson that challenged me the most, but it also gave me the greatest freedom. For me, it's about progress, not perfection.

If you, the reader, have learned anything, I hope you become aware of the need to go within, uncovering the shadow that dims your light. It takes courage to face the truth, but the truth will set you free.

And then you, too, can be the change you wish to see in the world.

Author's Note

My life journey is not over; in some ways, it has just begun. It is now that I must put into practice all the spiritual guidance, lessons, and truths I have learned. Irrefutable evidence that not only validated but was instrumental in my conviction regarding the truth about myself occurred when I cast my Chart of Origin from Caroline Myss's *Sacred Contracts*. It can only be calculated once, similar to your astrological birth chart.

Thoroughly reviewing all available archetypes, not counting the four survival ones, for eighteen months, I selected my twelve. It was simple and straightforward to cast my Archetypal Wheel. According to Myss's instructions, you are to "clear your mind of expectations and desires, and focus on your intention to be open to whatever guidance you receive. Take several deep breaths to clear your thoughts. Your archetypes will be guided into their appropriate houses by the energy of simultaneity, coincidence, spiritual order, divine paradox, and destiny."

To clear my mind, I took advantage of the meditation Caroline provides as a centering device. I closed my eyes and breathed deeply into my abdomen, allowing my stomach to expand as I breathed in and contract as I exhaled. I saw myself as a hollow reed, expanding and contracting. As I continued to take in slow, deep breaths, I repeated, "I have no desires. I have no thoughts. I am empty of all disturbances. I am empty of all my needs. I am open to receive."

I now felt ready to begin.

There are four steps to the process.

Step 1: Simple Preparation

Since I had the board game, I used the twelve cards corresponding to my archetypes, and the twelve cards numbered one through twelve. I kept them face down, the archetypes on my left, the numbers on my right.

Step 2: Intuitive Focus

I used the meditation from the book *Sacred Contracts* and followed the directions. First, I directed my attention entirely to my physical form. I then concentrated on the first chakra and visualized closing the shutters of that chakra to contain its energy entirely in my body. Feeling relief as I closed down any first-chakra concerns, I had a moment of peace, feeling held in one place.

Following the same process of closing the shutters for the remaining chakras, I began to enter a state where I viewed myself without any biases. By the time I came to my seventh chakra, it was the only opening in my body, making me entirely dependent on the energy of that spiritual portal.

Maintaining this divine state, I shuffled the stack of numbered cards, placing them back, face down. After mixing the archetype cards, I asked, "In which houses do these best serve me?" My intention attracted energy and created a magnetic circuit that directed them to their appropriate houses, as I worked with them in Step 3, reflecting the body of my contract.

Step 3: Intuitive Choice

Returning to the meditation, I pictured myself as a hollow reed, transmitting energy. From the facedown decks of cards, I drew a number and an archetype. The numbers correspond to the house into which that archetype should go. I wrote the name of each one into the numbered houses on my wheel.

Step 4: The Partnerships of Archetypes and Their Houses

After I placed all twelve cards on my wheel, I generated a unique energy field. Here, I animated the ley lines (the energetic lines that connect psychic power centers) between archetypes, houses, events, relationships, fears, love, and acts of grace: everything that encompasses the domain of my life. There are questions that facilitate this process. When I finished with the questions, I began to see clearly into all parts of my life, some of which I forgot, and some that were still in the shadow.

The casting of my Archetypal Wheel was instrumental in moving me forward. The truth was unfolding before me; I had adamantly stated, for the preceding six months, that the Addict archetype would fall into the First House, the house where the ego and personality reside. It's the house where I ask, "Who am I? Who is the person I show the world?" and it tells me what I am using to build my identity.

Halfway through casting my wheel, I pulled the number one card and subsequently turned over the Addict card. Chills and goose bumps coursed through my body, as I sat on the bed, stunned, not because I said it would and did, but because the truth was staring me in the face.

From first appearing at the age of five until twelve, the Addict was the persona I showed the world and was the dominant unconscious pattern of influence of my personality. It is my identity, and since 2000, when I got sober, it's the identity with which I lead. I am not anonymous and never was because I felt if I were open, I could help others. And I have.

The challenge for me was to have the strength to make my way without needing another's permission or approval and developing a keen sense of self. Throughout this book, you have witnessed this transformation, from the years of people-pleasing, wearing masks to gain acceptance from others, to my initiation and rebirth into a life that permanently removed those masks;

finally, I could stand in my center, liberated from the need for approval and validation from others.

I was free at last.

Bibliography and Recommended Reading

Bass, Ellen, and Laura Davis. *The Courage to Heal.*

Beattie, Melody. *The Language of Letting Go.*

Braden, Gregg. *Deep Truth, Fractal Time, The Spontaneous Healing of Belief.*

Canfield, Jack. *The Success Principles.*

Chopra, Deepak. *The Seven Spiritual Laws of Success, Super Brain, Creating Affluence.*

Chopra, Deepak, Debbie Ford, and Marianne Williamson. *The Shadow Effect, Course in Miracles Society. A Course in Miracles.*

Choquette, Sonia. *SOUL Lessons and Soul Purpose.*

Dass, Ram. *Polishing the Mirror.*

Dispenza, Dr. Joe. *You Are the Placebo.*

Dyer, Dr. Wayne. *The Power of Intention, Manifest Your Destiny, Wishes Fulfilled, The Shift, Being in Balance, Change Your Thoughts and Change Your Life.*

Grabhorn, Lynn. *Beyond the Twelve Steps.*

Hay, Louse. *You Can Heal Your Life.*

Hill, Napoleon. *Think and Grow Rich.*

Hoffman, Lois. *The Self-Publishing Roadmap, Write a Book, Grow Your Business.*

Holland, John. *Psychic Navigator, Power of the Soul, Born Knowing.*

Housden, Roger. *For Lovers of God Everywhere.*

Judith, Anodea. *Creating on Purpose, Chakra Yoga, Chakra Balancing.*

Katie, Byron. *Loving What Is.*

King, Deborah. *Truth Heals, Entangled in Darkness.*

Levine, Stephen. *A Year to Live.*

Myss, Caroline., *Anatomy of the Spirit, Sacred Contracts Entering the Castle, Why Some People Heal and Others Don't, Defy Gravity, Invisible Acts of Power.*

Nepo, Mark. *The Book of Awakening, Finding Inner Courage.*

Oman, Maggie. *Prayers for Healing.*

Pond, David. *Chakras for Beginners.*

Rich, Simona. *Third Eye Chakra.*

Richardson, Cheryl. *The Art of Extreme Self-Care.*

Ruiz, Don Miguel. *The Four Agreements, Beyond Fear, The Voice of Knowledge, The Mastery of Love, The Fifth Agreement.*

Simpson, Liz. *The Book of Chakra Healing.*

Silver, Tosha. *Change Me Prayers.*

Taylor, Madisyn. *Daily OM, Daily OM Learning to Live.*

Tolle, Eckhart. *A New Earth, The Power of Now.*

W., Bill. *The Big Book of Alcoholics Anonymous.*

Wauters, Ambika. *Chakras and Their Archetypes.*

Weiss, Dr. Brian. *Same Soul, Many Bodies.*

Williamson, Marianne. *A Return to Love.*

54077191R00136

Made in the
USA
Lexington, KY